SO-AEO-302

A Race Is a Nice Thing to Have

A Guide to Being a White Person or Understanding the White Persons in Your Life

Cognella Series on Advances in Culture, Race, and Ethnicity

A Race Is a Nice Thing to Have

A Guide to Being a White Person or Understanding the White Persons in Your Life

THIRD EDITION

JANET E. HELMS
Boston College

cognella®
SAN DIEGO

Bassim Hamadeh, CEO and Publisher
Amy Smith, Project Editor
Jess Estrella, Senior Graphic Designer
Sara Schennum, Licensing Associate
Alia Bales, Production Editor
Natalie Piccotti, Director of Marketing
Kassie Graves, Vice President of Editorial
Jamie Giganti, Director of Academic Publishing

Cover image copyright © 2018 iStockphoto LP/Pobytov.

Printed in the United States of America.

cognella® ACADEMIC PUBLISHING

3970 Sorrento Valley Blvd., Ste. 500, San Diego, CA 92121

Dedicated to my father, Brown J. Helms
(pronounced Hel-lems),
who continued to believe in White people enough
to try to re-educate them
throughout this lifetime.

Contents

Foreword

This Book Is a Critical Tool for Self-Awareness, Cultural Understanding, and Unity with Others

Dr. Janet Helms, Augustus Long Professor, at Boston College, has had an immense influence on the development of multiculturalism and social justice in both the American Counseling Association and the American Psychological Association. She is considered by many as the premier psychologist who has taught us to understand racism and social justice. She has received many awards for her writing, presentations, national influence, as well as having trained many outstanding psychology professionals.

Thus it is an honor to write outlining some of the issues she raises that I consider most important for societal understanding and eventual unity and tolerance among all peoples. Dr. Helms's approach to this is through examining issues of Whiteness and White identity. She shows how we can move from lack of tolerance and racism toward understanding and unity.

Through the lens of Whiteness and its meaning, Dr. Helms enables us all to see ourselves in a multicultural society ridden with racism and oppression. Systemically, she shows us how to improve ourselves and society. Not only Whites can learn from this book, but also People of Color, those of various socioeconomic groups, as well as anyone who considers themselves in some way a "minority."

The United States and its culture can no longer be defined as White. However today, most White people now identify as White more than ever. Many Whites have extended their definition of Whiteness to maintain power and control over non-White populations. At the same time, there are many Whites who identity as Whites, but use this knowledge for very different purposes. They understand the inherent privilege that comes with Whiteness, but wish to see others as equals where we all work together toward similar goals.

Thus we can think of two major categories of White people: one that wants to protect their White privilege, and another that still takes pride in their cultural background but is aware of the serious problem of racism. Regardless of the stage of identity and awareness, all of us can learn about developing increased tolerance and unity with others.

A Race Is a Nice Thing to Have explores both types of Whiteness. It offers an avenue for increasing communication and understanding between and among groups. The focus here is on helping people develop a positive White identity. At the same time, we learn more in depth about the group of White people that want to maintain the status quo. Identity development, as presented by Dr. Helms, can and will benefit all types of cultures and people.

Dr. Helms provides a clear path for all of us—White, People of Color, and others—to understand the process of racial and cultural identity development. Anyone who takes a serious look at this book will come away with a different and broader frame of mind. She or he may disagree with what is said here, but always there is new learning that ultimately will lead to a new future.

May I share a few bullet points of this action-based book that will make a difference in lives? You will learn:

1. How to make conversation about race visible, a topic from which many/most people run.
2. The relationship of social class and race. They are different but overlapping concepts.
3. Both the positive and potential negative aspects of the words "White" and "Black."
4. Issues of culture and White racism.
5. White identity development—here we see there are six levels of White identity. One can use this as a basis for developing a positive White identity.
6. The meaning of disintegration—the issues one often works through as they form a clearer basis of White identity. At the same time, disintegration may mean just that, the "White person wishes to stop or eliminate the possibility of integration."
7. Material and ideas for developing a positive White identity, which in turn have profound implications for all.

This is a superior book to complement many courses in the counseling and therapy curriculum—introduction, skills, theories, practicum. Students will have the opportunity to examine themselves and evaluate where they are in the whole concept of identity development. Students of Color will have the opportunity to understand the nature of Whiteness and its privilege more fully. In turn, these students will have an opportunity to examine their own identity development and develop their own theory of what it might mean for their own behavior and actions.

Allen E. Ivey, EdD, ABPP
Distinguished University Professor (Emeritus)
University of Massachusetts, Amherst
Board Certified in counseling psychology by the American Board of Professional Psychology

Preface

For racism to disappear in the United States, White people must take the responsibility for ending it. For them to assume that responsibility, they must become aware of how racism hurts White people and consequently, how ending it serves White people's interests. Moreover, this awareness not only must be accompanied by enhanced abilities to recognize the many faces of racism, but also by the discovery of options to replace it.

In this book, I intended to provide a perspective that would serve all four purposes. The perspective is intended to help White people (a) assume the proper responsibility for ending racism; (b) understand how racism impacts Whites as well as other racial groups; (c) present a model for analyzing racism as it is expressed by Whites; and (d) discover alternatives to racism as a means of coping with race in a multi-racial environment.

Therefore, it should be evident that I have written a book for White people. In this country, Whites seem to be the only racial group that spends more time and effort wondering about the implications of race for other groups than it does for itself. White people have difficulty accepting that they have a race and therefore are threatened by groups who have no such difficulties. Likewise, they seem to have no models for thinking about Whiteness as a healthy part of themselves rather than as a negative aspect of others. I have attempted to provide such a model.

In this book, I use a social definition of race as is the custom in this country. In other words, through custom, fiat, and law, a number of observable physical characteristics have come to be treated as factors denoting different "racial" groups. These characteristics include (but are not limited to) skin color of oneself or one's ancestors, presumed geographic region of origin, and primary language of oneself and/or one's ancestors.

Thus, in this book, when I use the concept "Whites" and "White culture," I am referring to those individuals who exhibit the physical characteristics of White Europeans and have been assimilated and acculturated into White Anglo-Saxon culture as it exists in the United States. Therefore, the contents of this book are intended for a special group of Whites and may not pertain to all Whites everywhere in the world and for all time.

"Race" is intended to be a self-help guide to better racial adjustment. Individuals who read it will approach the book from different levels of personal development and with different kinds of life experiences. Consequently, though some readers may be able to digest its content in a single gulp, others may find it more helpful to mull over each chapter, a bit at a time. Do not be surprised if strong emotions are aroused. Examining your emotions as they occur is a first step toward better racial adjustment.

In preparing the third edition of this book, I am particularly indebted to Susan Ginivisian for being a speed typist and for sharing with me her racial identity development issues as she typed. I am grateful to Amanda Weber, who saved me many times, as I looked for needed resources and for being the White person on my research team all the time. Kathy Flaherty offered her support and encouragement. Also, the rest of my research team (Kahlil DuPerry, Christina Douyon, Taylor Stewart, Eva Wilson, and Lianzhe Zheng) continually give me ideas for educational activities by sharing their real-life experiences. I owe a great deal of gratitude to Robert T. Carter, who has championed my theory and provided empirical support for it regardless of professional costs to himself. Also, I appreciate Allen Ivey's ongoing encouragement and willingness to write the foreword of this third edition of *A Race Is a Nice Thing to Have: A Guide to Being a White Person or Understanding the White Persons in Your Life*, and Elizabeth Robey, my former publisher, who helped make this edition possible.

Malcolm X argued that for racism to disappear, White people had to be re-educated to understand how racism lurks in their hearts. Since the first printing of this book, White scholars have begun to grapple with the issues of White racial identity development in many contexts, but there is still much work to be done and many White people to reach. This book represents my effort to further the work. I hope it is, at least in part, what Malcolm X intended.

Janet E. Helms
Institute for the Study and Promotion of Race and Culture
Boston College

1

The Meaning of Race in Society

Anthropologists have long argued that race is a meaningless term for describing people because any biological characteristics, assumed to be racial, that can be found in one supposed racial group can also be found in others. In the human genome era, through DNA analyses, scientists have discovered that a person's *physical appearance* reveals nothing about his or her ancestral origins, although it may mean something about how the person self-labels or is labeled by others.

But, you say, "I look different from people who are not White." The reality is that you look like some people who authorities label "White" and some people who authorities label something other than White. People who live together and mate together develop similar physical character-istics, which includes skin color. Historically, the matter of who should be considered White has been so confusing that race laws, social customs and policies were put into place to help society determine whether a person was White or not. Perhaps you have heard of the one-drop law wherein a person is defined as White if he or she has no known "drop" of African blood or ancestry.

But, you say, "I am Caucasian, I've always been Caucasian, and I always will be Caucasian." In other words, many people believe that Caucasian is a friendlier or more scientific synonym for Whites, but they are mis-taken. Many people believe that the origins of present day "Caucasians" are the Caucasus Mountains, but renowned historian Nell Irvin Painter's description of the evolution of the meaning of the Caucasian racial label suggests otherwise. At times, throughout history, Caucasian has referred to some Europeans, Eastern Asians, and Northern Africans, populations residing far outside of Caucasian regions. Moreover, historian Ronald Takaki reports that although Asian Indians and Whites in the US were once presumed to have the same ancestral origins, the Caucasus Mountains, by law, Caucasian is *not* a synonym for White because Caucasian actually refers to people who do not look White (Asian Indians) according to the "common [White] person." Power is the capacity, for example, to define people in or out of existence. Exercise 1.2 might help you figure out what Caucasian means to people using the label whether they know it or not.

To say that race or racial categories are not biological designations does not mean that biology or genetics does not determine a person's physical appearance. You inherited physical characteristics from your parents and they inherited physical characteristics from your grandparents and so on. Extended family members look alike. However, White people have the power to designate which physical similarities among people are "racial," what racial label should be assigned to them, and who has the power to count categories and make laws and policies pertaining to them. Moreover, the assignment of personality characteristics and behaviors to people, based on these factitious "racial" categories, supports ongoing racism in society.

Perhaps you are wondering why you should read an entire book about White people—even a short one. If race is such a fuzzy concept, why not just ignore it? The belief that racial categories matter is used to segregate White people from other people and to convince them that society's resources are their birthright exclusively. Unfortunately, society holds twin myths that people behave in desirable ways and deserve privileges if they are White, and people behave in undesirable ways and must earn privileges if they are not White. These myths are so firmly embedded in the U.S. society that it is necessary to address them directly if we want the harmful consequences of race to disappear and its positive aspects to remain. The following exercise illustrates how subtly the negativity of race is embedded in everyday conversation.

Exercise 1.1   Making the Invisible Conversation about Race Visible

Light skin color affords people many benefits and is considered a desirable aspect of personhood. Dark skin color is viewed negatively. This dichotomy is played out in everyday conversation where darkness is used as a synonym for bad things that happen. Consider the following excerpts. Can you tell what they mean?

> A news analyst states, "The Senator's good spin masks a darker reality."

> According to a music critic, "There's a little playfulness, but there's also a darker tone to his album."

> A reporter announces, "There is a dark new assessment by intelligence experts in Iraq."

> An actress in a TV drama: "I went through some really dark times. I really lost my way."

> A structural engineer: "The United States is in the dark ages where bridge inspection is concerned."

Try replacing "dark" or "darker" with a more descriptive adjective. Compare your list to someone else's list. Notice how much clearer communication is when people say explicitly what they mean rather than using symbolic language.

Now, notice how many times you hear dark or darkness used in everyday conversation. Try not to use the terms yourself for an entire week. Put aside a dollar for each time you slip and donate it to a worthy charity. Consider this your first step toward undoing symbolic racism.

Some White people believe that they can dissociate themselves from the burdens of guilt and responsibility associated with being White in the US. They do so by calling themselves "Caucasian." To be polite, some People of Color use the term as a euphemism for White.

Let us see what we can discover about the origins of the term from Nell Irvin Painter. For each item, circle True ("T") if you think it is an accurate account of the term Caucasian, according to historians and anthropologists, and False ("F") if you do not.

True	False	1. All of the White people who today call themselves "Caucasian" originally came from the Caucus Mountains (p. 3).
True	False	2. Anthropologists considered North Africans "Caucasians" (p. 80).
True	False	3. Caucasian referred to young, white enslaved women, who were physically attractive, submissive, and sexually available (p. 48).
True	False	4. Some Caucasians have been described as eating with their hands and relieving themselves in toilets near their food (p. 45).
True	False	5. The Greeks originally defined the Caucasian ethnic groups (p. 2).
True	False	6. When experts ranked the races along a hierarchy, Caucasians were always at the top of the ranking system (p. 86).
True	False	7. Celts, described as hidden, painted, strange barbarians, might have been ancestors of present day Europeans (p. 4).
True	False	8. Skin color has always been the primary criterion for determining races (p. 79).
True	False	9. Russians and Ukrainians trace their ancestry to illiterate Stone Age people who they believe were "racially pure" (p. 5).

Here are the answers: 9-T; 8-F; 7-T; 6-F; 5-T; 4-T; 3-T; 2-T; 1-F. The page numbers are from Painter's book. Race labeling is very complicated. Read her book before calling someone Caucasian so that you do not hurt his, her, or their feelings.

2

Social Class Is Not Race

Race is such an uncomfortable topic to acknowledge that White people try to find other terms to replace it. Social class is one concept that people often use for this purpose. Perhaps you have heard people say, "The only color that matters to me is green," meaning money. Possession of money is one definition of social class, but as shown in Table 2.1, social class means many different things to people. Table 2.1 shows indicators that social and behavioral scientists use to measure social class. Are they what you mean by social class?

Counseling psychologist William Ming Liu and associates found 448 terms that social and behavioral scientists have used to connote social class or SES. Perhaps it is evident that social class is an even more confusing concept than race is. To make the matter even more confusing, some authors recommend that it is necessary to differentiate social class from socioeconomic status (SES). According to this perspective, social class is the person's subjective evaluation of his or her own resources, whereas SES is the person's ranking according to societal indicators, such as education, occupation, and income.

Whether one calls the construct social class or SES, there is at least one way in which social class and race are similar. Assigning people to SES categories based on the types of observable criteria listed in Table 2.1 does not mean that members of the ascribed categories will behave in a similar manner. That is, just as is the case for race, one cannot tell anything about a person's likely personality characteristics or behaviors from the person's ascribed group membership.

Social class differs from race in many other ways. One way is its greater fluidity. Liu points out that people may consciously choose to change their social class. He uses as examples wealthy individuals who choose an impoverished lifestyle or corporate executives who give up lucrative positions for lower paying service jobs. Alternatively, people may aspire to move upward in social class by acquiring wealth, education, or prestigious positions. It is possible, though not necessarily easy, for individuals to change their social class by engaging in purposeful actions, but they can never really change their racial category.

For the most part, indicators of social class are external characteristics of the person's environment and can be observed or measured by the person himself or herself or by people in the outside world. In fact, prior to adulthood, a person has no social class of her or his own, but rather is defined by the people or resources around her or him. Race is imposed on the individual at the beginning of life, it has no observable traits or behaviors associated with it, but a person cannot change it through his or her own actions. In his book on the psychology of working, David Blustein points out that race, class, and gender interact as important influences in people's lives. Yet he warns against treating race and racism as "historical anachronisms" with no role in contemporary life.

Our task is to learn to differentiate social class from race. It is much easier to carry on a conversation about race or social class if the conversationalists are using the same words to mean the same concepts. Exercise 2.1 will help you think about classism in your life.

Exercise 2.1   Do You Engage in Classism?*

Classism may be defined as preferences, biases or discrimination directed toward individuals because of their perceived social class. Its function is to maximize one's economic resources as defined by the person's chosen social-class peer group. Liu defines the following four types of classism:

> Upward Classism: negative attitudes, beliefs about, or behaviors directed toward people that you believe have higher social-class standing than you.

---

*These definitions are adapted from William M. Liu, The social class-related experiences of men: Integrating theory and practice. *Professional Psychology: Research and Practice, 33, p. 357.*

Downward Classism: negative attitudes, beliefs about, or behaviors directed toward people that you believe have lower social-class standing than you.

Lateral Classism: negative attitudes, pressures, or behaviors associated with maintaining the same social-class standing as one's economic peers.

Internalized Classism: "feelings of anger, frustration, depression, despair, disappointment, and anxiety" that occur when the person cannot accomplish desired SES goals.

Start assessing your social class perceptions by responding to the following questions before you read the analysis of your answers at the bottom of the page.

1. What is your social class?

2. What factors identify you as belonging to that social class?

3. Do you have beliefs about people in higher social classes than yours? If so, list some of them.

4. Do you have beliefs about people in lower social classes than yours? If so, list some of them.

5. How do you determine whether other people belong to the same social class as you do?

6. Circle the following word(s) that best describe your feelings about your current social-class status: *satisfied content angry delighted resentful happy jealous depressed*

First, examine your answers to determine whether they reflect negative attitudes about people as described by Liu's classism categories. For example, if you listed stereotypes or negative attitudes in response to questions 3 and 4, then you may have tendencies to engage in upward or downward classism, respectively. Questions 1 and 2 should help you think about your social-class identity; that is, what factors you have learned to equate with social class. Lateral classism issues are assessed by questions 5 and 6.

Now for our purposes, differentiating social class from race, review your answers to questions 1 through 5 again and count the number of times you mentioned race as an aspect of social class. If you rarely mentioned race, then it is likely that you treat race and social class as different concepts. The more times you mentioned race in your answers, the more likely it is that you have merged the two concepts.

TABLE 2.1   Some of the Many Indicators of Social Class or Socioeconomic Status

Parents' Income	Own Income
Parents' Highest Level of Education	Own Highest Education Level
Parents' Occupation(s)	Own Occupation
Prestige of Parents' Occupation	Prestige of Own Occupation
Inherited Wealth	Self-Reported Social Class
Earned Wealth	Cultural Values
Eligibility for Free Lunch Programs	Political Power
Eligibility for Aid to Dependent Children	Life Style
Poverty	Marital Status
Census Track of Residence	Working Class
Census Track of School	Middle Class
Upper Class	Neighborhood Racial Composition
Zip Code	Telephone Ownership
Neighborhood Income Level	Human Capital
Social Capital	Resource Control
Welfare Recipient	Inner City
Barrio	Urban Poor
Upper Class	Employed
Culture of Poverty	Disadvantaged
Home Ownership	Car Ownership

3

Who Needs a Color-Blind Society?

For some time now, public officials, political leaders, educators, and otherwise sane people have been promoting the idea of a "color-blind" society. Depending somewhat upon whom one consults, such individuals seem to mean by this term, a society in which we pretend that we do not notice one another's skin-color. Leaving aside for the moment the fool-hardiness of this proposition, it seems to me to be not only an impossible goal, but an undesirable one as well. Moreover, some researchers have found that White people who endorse color blindness perspectives are more likely to engage in discrimination toward other racial groups, act in ways that preserve White privilege, and feel scared and helpless in interracial interactions when they are not in the majority.

Where does the thrust for the color-blindness movement come from? According to psychologist Helen Neville and associates, its origins can be traced back to the judicial system and scholarly debates about whether race does or is supposed to matter in our Constitution. She describes the four types of color-blindness summarized in Table 3.1.

At a general societal level, color-blindness is often promoted as a strategy for achieving social justice. This social justice rationale is most directly traceable to the Civil Rights movement of the 1960s and the Reverse Discrimination movement of the 1980s. A corollary of both has been that society has become conscious of the extent to which skin-color not only influences access to economic and political power, but also every person's day to day existence.

Individuals who advocate the Civil Rights form of color-blindness view it as a future status or ideal goal if you will—a way of denoting the ending of discrimination based on race. Most would agree that it does not exist yet, but they would also view it as a desirable state of being.

Persons who advocate the Reverse Discrimination form of color-blindness view it as a solution to real or imagined discrimination against White males, due to affirmative action programs. Thus, their position is generally, if one ignores race, then everyone will have access to the level of political and economic power in the society that they deserve. Interestingly, these color-blind advocates generally rely on Civil Rights leaders such as Martin Luther King to make their case. Thus, one frequently hears that King wanted people to be judged on their merit rather than their skin color.

In actuality, King did not advocate a policy of color-blindness, though he did demand civil equality regardless of skin-color. Nevertheless, he recognized that people come in different colors; otherwise, he would not have dreamed of "brown children" and "black children" and "white children" holding hands someday. He simply refused to believe that these differences in color made some people superior to others.

However, it should be possible and it is probably desirable for people to maintain and be proud of their respective colors without measuring one's self or others by it. In this country, color reminds one of one's history—how far one has come and how far one has to go and in what directions. This reminder need not be a bad thing unless we make it so.

Undoubtedly, each color we see in our society reminds us of some things we can be proud of as well as some things we would just as soon ignore. However, the shameful things will not disappear simply by pretending that color differences do not exist. Nor will they disappear if color is seen merely as a reminder of ancestral guilt. Rather color-related guilt and shame disappear by making amends for what one has done wrong with respect to color differences in the past, making sure that one does not permit these trespasses to occur in the present, and moving on with one's life.

Moving on should mean that we accept our skin-color as an integral part of who we are. The things people ignore or pretend do not exist are usually scary, unpleasant, or distasteful. Our skin-colors do not belong in that category. If you think about it, the ranges of skin-color we have in the United States are beautiful and remarkable. It is what we do about them that is unsavory.

TABLE 3.1 Some Types of Color Blindness

Type and Description	Examples of Relevant Attitudes or Behaviors
Invisibility of Race—refusal to notice racial group membership for fear of being perceived as prejudiced against other racial groups.	"I don't notice what race people are. Everyone is the same to me."
Color-Evasion—rejecting the myth of White superiority and associated racism by emphasizing the ways in which White people's experiences are the same as those of People of Color.	"I don't know why you have to be a hyphenated-identity. Why can't you just be American like me?"
Power-Evasion—endorsement of the belief that everyone has the same opportunities regardless of race.	"My great grandparents did not have any education or money when they came to this country, but they became the wealthiest people in their community. They pulled themselves up by their bootstraps. Why can't you people?"
Race as Taboo—by not talking about race, one avoids creating a hostile climate, and taking personal responsibility.	If I said that "I'm proud to be White, people would think that I'm a member of some White hate group."

These types of color-blindness were adapted from Helen Neville et al., (2000), Construction and validation of the Color-Blind Racial Attitudes Scale (CoBRAS), Journal of Counseling Psychology, 47, p. 60.

4

I'm Not Colored!

White people are raised to be confused about their own color. While they are taught to be aware of other people's color, polite White persons do not mention color in public—especially their own. Dare to mention that a person is White if you are not and you become a racist or a nationalist or (heaven forbid) a separatist. Dare to mention White if you are, and you become a supremacist at worst and an uncouth braggart at best.

Why are White people so uncomfortable about acknowledging color? Because from the time they are capable of recognizing color differences, around age three or four years, they are bombarded with ambiguous messages about color. Consider the following situation: Three-year-old Sally Jane points to a brown or black person in a store and says, "Oh look, mommy, at the chocolate man. Can I bite him?" Or perhaps she exclaims in that loud child's voice guaranteed to make parents cringe in dismay, "Why is that man so dirty?" What would you do?

Many parents would shush her embarrassedly and rush her out of the person's presence. From this exchange, Sally Jane begins to learn that color is a handicap, a physical impairment in the language of the day. One notices physical disabilities, but one certainly does not let the impaired person know that one does. Thus, Sally Jane begins to learn to pretend that she does not see skin-color whenever she sees it.

Other parents might attempt to enlighten Sally by explaining that "some people were left in God's oven longer than others." From this intervention, Sally Jane learns that White is the best color to be and there is something wrong with persons who are other than White.

Still other parents might carefully explain to Sally Jane that "people come in different colors, and the man can't help being the color he is. So, we mustn't make him feel uncomfortable." Of course, Sally Jane learns from this explanation that color is a deficit and that Whiteness is an asset.

As Sally Jane matures, the superiority of her Whiteness over color is hammered into her consciousness. She learns that white is "pure," "clean," and "angelic." She learns that dark is "bad," "evil," and "satanic." There are few positive images in the English language associated with black. There are legions of positive images associated with white. Just to discover how much color differentials have slipped into your unconsciousness, try the following exercise.

Exercise 4.1   What Is White?

Fill in as many words or phrases under each column as you can in about five minutes. Don't spend too much time thinking or censoring your thoughts, just write whatever comes to mind. Each column has one entry to get you started.

White		Black	
1 Positive Characteristics	2 Negative Characteristics	3 Positive Characteristics	4 Negative Characteristics
Snow	Bland	In the black	dirty

When you have finished, notice the differences in the lengths of your lists. Chances are that if you are like most people, you were able to generate many items for columns 1 and 4, but not for columns 2 and 3. The superiority of white is embedded into our language.

At the same time that Sally Jane is being taught that the essence of White is superiority, she is also learning that the color white is a deficit. In school she learns that white is "the absence of all color." And so, she and her peers begin a lifelong quest to obtain color by baking themselves in the sun. They have begun to define their whiteness according to what they are not. They are people without color.

Why the condition of being White is so disgusting to many White people is puzzling. Psychiatrist Frances Cress Welsing explained it as an unconsciously motivated discomfort with the recessive gene that resulted in reduced skin pigmentation, that is, the person is trying to overcome a color disability.

An environmental explanation is that White as a skin-color symbolizes power and oppression in this country. White is the skin color of the people who historically have conquered, enslaved, and oppressed People of Color. It would not be surprising if many White people become uncomfortable when they think of themselves as "looking like" a member of the aggressive group.

Still others are exaggeratedly proud of their Whiteness. They do not only think that "White is beautiful," they think it is superior. Relying on a characteristic over which one had no control as the foundation of one's self-worth places the person at risk. If society ever evolves to a point where skin colors are not differentially evaluated, the person who defines himself or herself primarily on the basis of color will have lost a sense of self as well as self-worth. Consequently, one generally finds skin color supremacists aggressively pursuing social policies of color separation and White domination. In their minds, they have a lot to lose—themselves.

Although the White person may choose a variety of ways of dealing with being White, it is clear that the messages one receives about it are ambiguous. One should marry White, live in White neighborhoods and so forth, but one is not supposed to consciously acknowledge that one is White unless one is a bigot. So, in this society, one learns to act White, but not to be White. White people teach each other to lie about being White.

5

But What Color Am I?

White! White! WHITE! Try describing yourself out loud as White. Several researchers and consultants in race relations have observed that White people have difficulty admitting that they are White. When asked their race, they may respond in terms of their nationality, American, or a specific ethnicity such as Italian, Irish, Jewish, Polish, or in many cases "mutt" or "mongrel," the latter meaning that the White person speaking has lost her or his links to a specific ethnic past, probably by means of acculturation and assimilation.

When challenged about their "White flight," most respondents will argue "but I *am* German (or Irish or whatever fills the blank best)." However, the reality is that one does not have either ethnic heritage or racial heritage. In truth, the decision to be positively White need not be an either/or decision. One generally has both—a race and an ethnicity—whether or not one is consciously aware of them. What the White ethnic groups have in common is that they are all White as defined by society.

As White people, they all have access to White privilege at some level. That is, regardless of what socioeconomic level one observes, Whites are more advantaged than most People of Color of the same socioeconomic level. White privilege is a benefit of being White and is the foundation of racism.

In exchange for abandoning or appearing to abandon their ethnic roots, White predecessors in the country permit each wave of White immigrants access to White privilege at some level. Each new White child is born with similar access. That is, White culture assimilates or accepts them. Being accepted as White requires White people to acculturate to White culture where acculturate means to learn the rules, customs, and principles of Whiteness. If one acculturates or appears to do so in public, then one is accepted in many White environments. Therefore, acculturation to White culture is a benefit of being White *for White people*.

In describing White culture, counselor educator John Axelson observed that it derives from the Anglo-Saxon groups who resettled the country prior to the 1880s and the subsequent White immigrants who subscribed to the customs that existed when they arrived here. Psychologist Judy Katz pointed out that White culture is characterized by specific customs, attitudes, and beliefs. Some of these are summarized in Table 5.1.

TABLE 5.1   Some Aspects of White Culture

Some Societal Dimensions	Expressions
Rugged Individualism—The individual is the most important societal unit.	People should take care of themselves; individual achievement is most valued.
Nuclear Family—An "ideal" family is defined as two parents and children.	Alternative family structures (e.g., single parents, extended families) are considered deviant.
Rationalism—mind, body, and emotions should be treated as separate entities.	People who express emotions in "rational" situations (e.g., political speeches) are devalued.
Time—time is perceived as a quantity.	People are expected to save time, spend time, and perform on time.
European Aesthetics—beauty is defined by European standards.	People cut, dye, and starve themselves to resemble the European ideal of beauty.
Action Orientation—Everyone is responsible for what happens to her/him and controls one's own fate.	If people are homeless, it is because they want to be.
Universalism—the normative and best characteristics are defined by European culture.	Introduction of multicultural curricula in schools necessarily means a diluted education.
Competition—the society's resources belong to the best.	Access to societal goods is determined by competition as reflected in test scores.
History—the most important American history is White.	Separate weeks, months, and so forth are needed to teach about other groups.

Although White culture is a minority culture in the world, it is the dominant or host culture in the United States. White people's adherence to White culture has allowed White people to survive and thrive. It is an important part of White identity albeit an unconscious part.

However, it ought to be possible to accept one's Whiteness and partake of White culture without also insisting upon maintaining the benefits of racism for oneself and other Whites. In other words, learning to be comfortable as a White person requires the following steps: (1) making a decision to abandon racism, (2) observing the ways in which racism is maintained in your environments, (3) learning the differences between expression of racism and expression of White culture, and (4) discovering what is positive about being White.

These four White awareness steps are harder than they seem. To make a decision to abandon racism means one must be willing to acknowledge the ways in which one has been a racist or benefits from it. To observe the ways in which racism is maintained requires that one not only be aware that racism exists on some abstract level, but in specific, observable, concrete ways. Given that White culture is often invisible to its partakers, it is sometimes difficult to notice when it is being imposed on others as "the best" culture.

Likewise, it may be difficult to discover what is positive about being White given that "White" and "racist" are often treated as synonyms and that there are few positive White racial role models. Thus, the last step may be the most difficult to accomplish and may account for why some White people feel angry when members of other racial groups are allowed to have a race, but Whites are not. Exercise 5.1 may help you discover whether you are in need of positive White identity racial role models.

Find a sheet of paper and a writing utensil. Set your timer for two minutes. Now, without censoring your thoughts, write down as many answers as you can to the following question:

"What do you like about being White?"

Now go through your answers and cross out all of the responses that (1) involve comparing yourself to other racial groups; (2) use variants of the word "racist"; (3) involve defining yourself according to what you are not. Count the number of items remaining. This is your White identity score and is an indicant of how you view yourself as a White person. Here is an example of how responses might be scored.

Answer	Disposition
1. *I'm not a racist.*	Cross this one out (see #1, 2, & 3)
2. *Whites are the majority.*	Cross this one out (see #1)
3. *I'm not Black.*	Cross this one out (see #1)

Thus, this person would receive a score of zero, which means that he or she could not think of any positive consequences of being White.

I have encountered few White people who score higher than 1 on this exercise, and most score zero. So, if you scored higher than one, then you are probably more advanced with respect to White identity development than your White counterparts. However, if you re-examine your remaining responses when you have read the rest of the book, you may learn something about yourself.

6

Recognizing Racism

A person does not have to be a racist or indulge in racism if he or she is consciously White. These terms are not synonyms. *The American Heritage Dictionary* defines racism as: "The notion that one's own racial stock is superior."

Social psychologist James Jones argues that there are three basic forms of racism. One form is individual, the extent to which one holds attitudes, beliefs, feelings, and/or engages in behaviors that promote one's own racial group as superior. Another is cultural, defined as the unrealistic positive evaluation of the cultural products and achievements of one's own racial group while actively ignoring or denigrating those of other groups. Institutional involves rules, regulations, laws, and social policies and customs designed to maintain the superior or dominant status of one's own racial group over another.

Each type of racism can exist overtly or covertly. For instance, one can use racial slurs oneself or just not intervene when others do. Likewise, each type may be expressed intentionally or unintentionally. One does not have to intend to have expressed racism in order to have done so.

Some examples of each kind of racism, described by John Axelson, are presented in Table 6.1. The list is not meant to be exhaustive. Nor are the categories and examples mutually exclusive.

TABLE 6.1 Examples of Different Forms of Racism

Type: Individual

General Characteristics	Societal Expression
Belief in superiority of Whites	Violence against "non-Whites"; making fun of physical characteristics or customs of "non-White" groups; racial harassment; laughing at racist jokes
Denial of the existence of racism in any form	Nonsupport of race-related civil rights legislation; uncritical acceptance of all-White work environments
Belief that lack of success of "non-White persons" is due to genetic inferiority or racial-group malaise	Using derogatory racial epithets; unthinking adherence to "bootstrap" philosophy; unwillingness to support race-related affirmative action; promulgation of racial stereotypes

Type: Cultural

General Characteristics	Societal Expression
Language superiority	Limiting access to work and education to "standard" (read White) English speakers
Law, politics defined from a White perspective	Black political candidates are assumed to be "Black leaders," but White candidates are not "White leaders"
In education, science, philosophy and so forth, the contributions of White people are the best	Contributions of other racial groups are invisible; products (e.g., music, literature, ideas) of these groups are "better" when presented by a White person

Type: Institutional

General Characteristics	Societal Expression
Law enforcement policies are more stringent for People of Color	Police brutality; stopping people in the "wrong" neighborhood; severe sentences for the same crimes
Unemployment and underemployment for People of Color	Unemployment rate of Blacks has been at least three times the White rate; Asians do not necessarily hold jobs commensurate with their educational levels
Inadequate housing	Discriminatory pricing; mortgage loan discrimination; segregation of housing by race

White people in this country *did* invent racism in its various manifestations. Its origins can be traced back to Columbus's decision that the "red-skinned" occupants he found in the Americas were his property to transport, sell, and kill. This philosophy of the inferiority of People of Color was even more clearly stated in the Constitution where Black men were treated as three-fifths of a person, and consequently had no rights. Racism was designed to benefit White people. (Chances are that if People of Color had invented it, they would not have placed themselves at the bottom of the socio-political hierarchy.) Whereas some attempts have been made to reduce the racism inherent in broken treaties, racially restrictive legislation, and so forth, *White people have not been educated about the meaning and costs to them* of maintaining White privilege as the spoken or unspoken law of the land. Until this lesson is learned, it is unlikely that racism will disappear and the development of psychologically healthy White people remains problematic.

In brief, the major cost to White people is that the perpetuation of racism makes it virtually impossible to function and compete in a multiracial society except through domination, suppression, and massive denial of reality. However, some White people have evolved to a state where these modes of interacting with other people are perceived as morally bereft. Such people find themselves caught in a quandary—to acknowledge the unfairness of things risks ostracism from the White group, but to carry on business as usual creates a schism within oneself. On one side is the moral self; on the other side is the socialized White self.

Writers, such as Judy Katz and Audrey Thompson, have noted the high levels of guilt, anger, and anxiety that accompany the two faces of Whiteness. Many White people manage these feelings by denying the existence of racism as a White phenomenon and/or their part in it as White people. However, denial is a fragile coping strategy. Some manage their feelings of discomfort by distancing themselves from other Whites by claiming an oppressed ethnicity, social class, or sexual orientation instead of their White racial group membership. These forms of managing uncomfortable feelings work to some extent as long as the person is not forced to confront reality. But as the society becomes more obviously multiracial, it is likely that many White people will find themselves "defenseless" as they are forced to recognize the implications of being White in a multi-colored society.

Psychologist Jean Phinney has found that, unlike other racial groups, few White people of various ages seem to be asking themselves questions about what it means to be White. Nevertheless, to the extent that they do engage in such self-exploration, their self-esteem seems to be high. Perhaps facing the feared subject allows one to come to terms with it. In my book, *"Black and White Racial Identity,"* I argue that development of a positive, psychologically healthy White racial identity *requires* a conscious decision to abandon racism. This first step toward abandonment of racism requires recognition of racism in its many forms as well as the ways in which Whites individually and collectively benefit from it. In Table 6.1, how many of the examples of the societal expressions of racism did you recognize? How many have you observed and/or participated in in your daily life?

The tricky part of recognizing one's own participation in racism is that it may be more subtle than the examples shown in Table 6.1. Social psychologists Samuel Gaertner and John Davidio have conducted many years of research by which they have shown that many White people believe in the equality of all people. Moreover, if asked, they would likely say that they do not discriminate against People of Color, but they still—perhaps not consciously—hold negative racial stereotypes and beliefs about People of Color that influence their outgroup behaviors in a racially biased manner. Gaertner and Davidio call this process "aversive racism." In Exercise 6.1, I attempt to make aversive racism more visible to you.

Exercise 6.1   Recognizing Aversive Racism

The key ingredients of aversive racism are as follows: (1) the White person endorses fair and equitable treatment of all racial groups, but unconsciously holds feelings of anxiety, guilt, or fear towards Blacks (or other People of Color). (2) Because of uncomfortable feelings, the White person attempts to avoid interacting with members of the catalyst group or to terminate such interactions quickly, if the interactions are not avoidable. (3) The White person engages in subtle, indirect, or not conscious racist acts in an effort to cope with feelings of discomfort and avoid being perceived as racist, which would be incongruent with his or her equalitarian philosophy. (4) The White person wants to avoid thinking bad thoughts, experiencing feelings of discomfort, and discriminating against the focal group in order to preserve an image of oneself as not racist.

Following are some examples of blatant racist acts as described in Table 6.1 or *micro inequities*, defined as small, subtle, or indirect cross-racial acts that People of Color report experiencing on a regular basis. First, decide what type of act (blatant or micro) the example represents, and then explain why it occurred. What motivated the White person to act in the manner described?

The Action	Type	Motivation for the Action
1. A White person locks the car door when he or she sees a Black person approaching.		
2. A White woman clutches her purse to her side when a Black woman enters an elevator.		
3. A White employer finds a grammatical error in a report written by an Asian employee and recommends that the person obtain remedial English lessons.		
4. An employer searches for "qualified" minority employees, but not "qualified" White employees.		
5. White people ask an Asian American woman what country she was born in and refuse to believe that she is American.		
6. Cab drivers refuse to stop for Black people.		
7. Wait persons in restaurants give the check to the person with the lightest skin color.		
8. A predominately White university admissions committee routinely admits White students with low test scores, but does not admit Latinos/Latinàs with low test scores because the committee wants to protect them from failure.		

Did you recognize that all of the actions are examples of aversive racism as manifested through micro inequities? These are all acts that can be justified as not racist by a White person engaging in them. That is, the person can generate rational explanations for why he or she behaved in the described manner, but these explanations are often consistent with the examples of blatant racism shown in Table 6.1.

From my above list of key ingredients, Actions 1, 4, 6, 7, and 8 are examples of avoiding or prematurely terminating interactions (#2); Actions 2 and 3 are examples of subtle not conscious acts of bias (#3); Action 5 is an example of preserving a non-racist self-image.

Each of the actions is based on differentiating "we" (White people) from "them" (not White people). The way to overcome aversive racism is to make explicit one's biases and then actively attempt to counteract them. That is, one needs to take active steps to turn them into us by recognizing common goals or human conditions.

7

A Model of White Identity Development

I magine that your daughter or best female friend (or whoever functions in that role for you) announces one day, "Surprise, I'm getting married to someone of another race!" What do you think? What do you feel? What do you say to her? Now, she says, "Oops! I made a mistake; I am getting married, but it's to someone of *our* race." What do you think, feel, and say?

Examine your responses. Did your reactions to the situations change? Chances are they did. But it does not matter if they did not. Racial identity theory deals with how you perceive yourself as a racial being (Who did you think of when she said "our race?") as well as how you perceive others racially (Who represents "another race" to you?). One's thoughts, feelings, and behaviors are influenced by how one "identifies" with respect to racial matters.

What did you say to your daughter/friend? What did you feel? Probably, you noticed that each of these dimensions—feelings, attitudes, and behaviors—can be positive, negative, or somewhere in the middle. Perhaps you were also surprised to notice the quality and/or intensity of your reactions. Racial identity theory in general attempts to provide a framework for understanding these reactions. White racial identity theory attempts to provide a framework that makes sense in light of the socialization and common life experiences of White people.

In my model of White racial identity development, I suggest that a healthy White identity potentially develops via a two phase process, internalization of racism and evolution of a nonracist White identity. Each of these phases is hypothesized to consist of three schemas. Think of a racial-identity schema as a pair of eyeglasses or contact lenses through

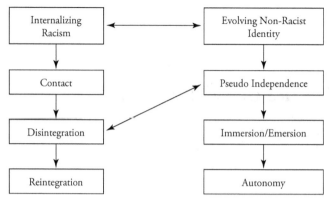

FIGURE 7.1a **A Model of White Identity Development**

which the person perceives or reacts to racial aspects of oneself as well as events in one's social contexts. The schemas are not mutually exclusive. So, just as a person may wear more than one pair of eyeglasses (e.g., prescription glasses and sunglasses) at a time, so too may the person use more than one schema at a time to react to racial issues.

Nevertheless, most people have a preference—the schema that works best for them or that they are accustomed to using. In this chapter, I will briefly present the structure of the model. In subsequent chapters, I will present a more detailed discussion of each schema. Figure 7.1a illustrates the components of the model.

The Contact schema is the foundation of White identity. Engagement in the process of developing a nonracist identity requires individuals to overcome the natural tendency of White people to be oblivious or neutral toward racial issues because of their privileged status. Schemas, characterized as internalizing racism (Contact, Disintegration, and Reintegration) are used to maintain the status quo. Schemas characterized as critical to the evolution of a nonracist White identity (Pseudo Independence, Immersion/Emersion, and Autonomy) require challenging some aspect of White racial socialization norms. Often feelings associated with Disintegration serve as catalysts for this evolution.

In this country, every White person is born into or immigrates into a society in which it is better to be perceived as White than not. This norm is a racist orientation. However, it is so subtle, pervasive, and ever present that it is possible for White people to ignore or deny it. To the extent that this denial persists, it is not possible to develop a healthy White non-racist identity though, in truth, many White people seem to function quite well without one. The internalization of racism phase involves internalization of the rules of racism and the evolution of self-protective strategies to maintain the benefits of White privilege.

The first schema of White identity development is Contact. Contact is characterized by an innocence, ignorance, or neutrality about race and racial issues. The person is not consciously White and assumes that other people are "raceless," too, with the exception of minor differences in coloration. Contact people generally present a picture of either naïve curiosity or timidity about other races. Contact ceases to be an effective schema when the person is forced to face the political implications of race in this country. Alternatively, in a personally meaningful situation, the person may reach a level of maturity that allows the person to understand the consequences to a White person of offending other Whites. Contact is disrupted if the person cannot find a way to avoid or lessen the internal tension that arises because of this new awareness. The primary self-protective strategy of the Contact schema is denial or "color blindness." One can continue to react to events through the Contact schema as long as one can pretend that race does not matter.

The second schema of White identity is Disintegration. The person uses this schema when denial no longer works. The general theme of this schema is confusion. It occurs because the person consciously acknowledges that he or she is White and that certain benefits accrue from belonging to the White membership group, which are at risk. These benefits include kinship with a group that shares common cultural characteristics and membership in the most politically, socially, and economically powerful racial group. Recognition of these benefits carries with it an awareness of the negative consequences of their potential loss, and awareness that maintaining uncontested membership in the White group requires one to treat other racial groups immorally.

Thus, when using the Disintegration schema, the person is caught in the midst of a moral dilemma(s), to be loved, valued, and respected by other White people, he or she must subscribe to immoral social practices, but to conform to them denies the common humanity of all people. Since this quandary is painful to one's psyche, the person often resolves it by distorting reality. That is, the person learns to blame the victims of racism. Accordingly, a Person of Color cannot be treated unjustly because people only get what they deserve and/or earn; if they do not have anything, then they did not earn anything. Therefore, it is a just world after all!

As the person's system of distortion becomes more complex, he or she develops the capacity to use the Reintegration schema. When using this schema, the person is not only consciously White, but considers Whites to be superior to all other racial groups. In the two previous schemas, the person must contend with the imperfections and contradictions of Whiteness and, consequently, of oneself as a White person. As an emollient to one's wounded self-esteem, he or she denigrates, appropriates, and ignores the contributions to the society of groups other than Whites. Thus, the primary self-protective strategy during this schema is displacement or scapegoating; that is, resolving one's inner turmoil by blaming People of Color for one's condition rather than Whites.

Because they belong to the politically dominant group, White people can generally use the Reintegration schema forever, if they wish. Each new racial incident can easily be explained via displacement, or blaming the Person of Color. Ceasing to rely on this schema probably requires a catastrophic event or a series of personal encounters that the person can no longer ignore. That is, her or his moral conscious, abandoned during Disintegration, must be re-awakened. This moral re-awakening both ends the racism phase and begins the nonracist or anti-racist White identity phase.

The first schema of the second phase of White identity development is Pseudo-Independence. Use of this schema is characterized by the person's maintenance of a positive view of Whiteness, which is scaled down to more realistic proportions. That is, the person is no longer invested in maintaining the belief that White is superior or perfect, though he or she does not yet have a new belief system to replace previous socialization. To replace the old beliefs, the person might adopt White liberalist views in which it is assumed that People of Color can be helped to become the equal of Whites through such activities as affirmative action programs, special education programs, and so forth. The primary self-protective strategies of this schema are intellectualization and denial. That is, on an intellectual level the person recognizes the political implications of race in this country, but he or she still denies or does not consciously admit the responsibility of Whites in general and oneself as a White person for maintaining racism.

Pseudo-Independence is also probably a pretty stable schema because the person who uses it effectively is likely to receive positive reinforcement from other Whites who are seeking a new way to be White, as well as People of Color who likely think that this kind of White is better than most of the others that they have encountered. However, use of the Pseudo-Independence schema exposes the White person to the realities that White liberalism does not rid the environment of racism or its consequences, and that many People of Color do not want to be White and/or assimilate into White culture. If such messages consistently slip through the person's protective coping strategies, then she or he develops the potential to use the fifth schema of White identity, Immersion-Emersion.

Immersion-Emersion is characterized by an effort to understand the unsanitized version of White history in the United States. It involves an active exploration of racism, White culture, and assimilation and acculturation of White people. When using this schema, the person assumes personal responsibility for racism and develops a realistic awareness of the assets and deficits of being White. The moral re-education of other White people is a central theme of this schema. Sensitization is the primary self-protective strategy as the person actively seeks out experiences with other Whites that will help her or him understand the meaning of being White, and thereby grow beyond racism.

Realistic self-appraisal forces the White person to confront the loneliness and isolation of being a consciously positively White person in a White society that denies and distorts the significance of race and the societies of Peoples of Color, which have historically based reasons to be suspicious of consciously White people. As a means of reducing her or his own isolation, the person searches for opportunities to actively confront racism, as well as analogous forms of oppression in her or his environment. Moreover, he or she seeks within race and cross-racial experiences that permit the person to develop an equalitarian or humanitarian attitude toward people regardless of their race. Thus, confrontation, inclusion, and collectivism are the primary self-protective strategies of this last schema, Autonomy. Additionally, Autonomy is a schema in which the person feels safe and secure within oneself when he or she engages in experiences to nurture her or his Whiteness as personally defined.

Exercise 7.1 will give you an opportunity to examine the extent to which you are predisposed toward the various schemas. Attitudes, behaviors, and emotions do not necessarily evolve at the same rate. Presumably, the greater the difference between the three, the more internal racial tension the person is likely to experience.

It should also be noted that I intend the phases of identity to reflect fluid, changeable constructs rather than discrete, linear, stepwise mutually exclusive stages. Thus, if the analogy of eyeglasses does not adequately capture the fluidity of stages for you, perhaps it might be more appropriate to think of the schemas as levels of liquids of different weights (e.g., oil and water) contained in a cylinder (the person) as illustrated in Figure 7.2.

Thus, each person may have different levels of each type of schema, ranging from none to the full volume of the cylinder. If we think of the levels as fluids, then levels of the schemas may evaporate or expand depending on the person's (racial) life experiences. Thus, the exact levels present in any individual depend on the combination of when one shakes the cylinder (e.g., race-related events), maturational level, life experiences, and environmental circumstances. When one shakes the cylinder, whatever schemas of identity are present disperse. Thus, at any particular time, one might expect the person to react from whatever schema is dominant (has the highest level) and/or is at the top of her or his racial identity cylinder when a relevant event occurs.

So, for example, suppose the person whose schemas of identity are illustrated in Figure 7.2a hears that the Civil Rights Act was not signed (a race-related event). Since the person's Contact aspects are strongest (e.g., the highest level), then this person will likely react in a way that is consistent with the Contact schema as previously (and subsequently) described.

Thus, statements such as "Why do Blacks want a Civil Rights Law?" or "I thought racial discrimination ended a long time ago" would be reflective of the naiveté of high levels of Contact. Before you continue reading, try filling in the blank cylinder in Figure 7.2b to illustrate which levels of White identity flow in you and how strongly.

Exercise 7.1A   Workshop Activity on Self-Assessing White Racial Identity

For each of the subsequent items, use the following scale to indicate the extent to which the item is true of you.

1 – Strongly Disagree   2 – Disagree   3 – Agree   4 – Strongly Agree

Write the numbers of your responses on the line next to the item. Add together your responses to the items preceded by the same combination of letters and plot your scores on the graph. Draw one line to connect the totals preceded by double letters (e.g., CB) and another to connect the totals preceded by single letters (e.g., C). This will give you a racial identity profile.

C1.   _____   There is no race problem in the United States

C2.   _____   My race is the human race.

C3.   _____   I personally do not notice what race a person is.

_____   C TOTAL

CB1. _____ If I am asked to describe a person, I would not or do not mention the person's race.

CB2. _____ I have or would dress like people from other cultures.

CB3. _____ I do not discuss the characteristics of White people in public settings.

_____ CB TOTAL

D1. _____ American society is sick, evil, and racist.

D2. _____ There is nothing I can do to prevent racism.

D3. _____ I avoid thinking about racial issues.

_____ D TOTAL

DB1. _____ I left or would leave the country to escape racism

DB2. _____ I do not discuss "touchy" racial issues.

DB3. _____ I avoid people who talk about race.

_____ DB TOTAL

R1. _____ I believe that White culture or Western civilization is the most highly developed, sophisticated culture to have ever existed on earth.

R2. _____ Africans and Blacks are more sexually promiscuous than Europeans and Whites.

R3. _____ The White race will be polluted by intermarriage with Blacks.

_____ R TOTAL

RB1. _____ When a Black male stranger sits or stands next to me in a public place, I move away from him.

RB2. _____ I live or would live in a segregated (White) neighborhood.

RB3. _____ The people I do my non-business related socializing with either are Whites or Blacks who "act White."

_____ RB TOTAL

P1. _____ I identify with my ethnic group, social class, or other disadvantaged group rather than the White racial group.

P2. _____ I believe that affirmative action programs should be used to give minorities opportunities.

P3. _____ White people should help Black people become equal to Whites.

_____ P TOTAL

PB1. _____ I have invited a minority person over to my house for dinner.

PB2. _____ For Martin Luther King's Birthday, I attend or would voluntarily attend a commemorative event.

PB3. _____ I have tried to help Whites understand Blacks.

_____ PB TOTAL

E1. _____ White culture and society must be restructured to eliminate racism and oppression.

E2. _____ Whites and White culture are not superior to Blacks and Black culture.

E3. _____ A multi-cultural society cannot exist unless Whites give up their racism.

_____ E TOTAL

EB1. _____ I have studied the history of White and Western European people.

EB2. _____ I meet with Whites to discuss our feelings and attitudes about being White and White racism.

EB3. _____ I have voluntarily participated in activities to help me overcome my racism.

_____ EB TOTAL

A1. _____ I accept that being White does not make me superior to any other racial group.

A2. _____ Being a member of a multi-racial environment is a must for me.

A3. _____ My Whiteness is an important part of who I am.

_____ A TOTAL

AB1. _____ I speak up in a White group situation when I feel that a White person is being racist.

AB2. _____ I express my honest opinion when a Black person is present without worrying about whether I appear racist.

AB3. _____ I live in a multi-racial community.

_____ AB TOTAL

These workshop items are not from a validated scale and are presented here for the reader's possible self-exploration. Abbreviations are C = Contact attitudes, CB = Contact behavior, R = Reintegration attitudes, RB = Reintegration behavior, D = Disintegration attitudes, DB = Disintegration behavior, P = Pseudo-Independent attitudes, PB = Pseudo-Independent behavior, E = Emersion attitudes, EB = Emersion behavior, A = Autonomy attitudes, AB = Autonomy behavior. Higher scores indicate higher levels of attitudes/behaviors.

This exercise is adapted from Janet E. Helms (Ed.), *Black and White Racial Identity: Theory, Research, and Practice* (pp. 63–64). CT: Greenwood Press.

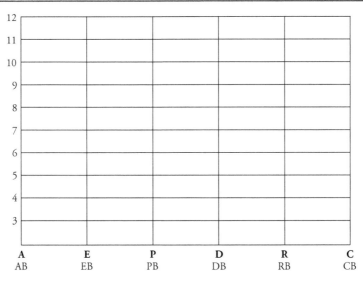

FIGURE 7.1b Attitudinal/Behavior Levels. Higher scores indicate levels of attitudes/ behaviors. Places where your attitudinal and behavior lines do not converge may reveal problem areas in your White identity development.

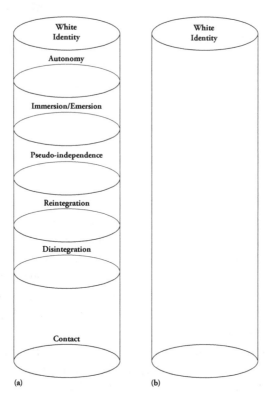

FIGURE 7.2 Think about racial identity schemas as different levels and types of liquids within a container. The cylinder on the left (7.2a) represents an individual whose contact characteristics are most strongly developed. Mark the cylinder on the right (7.2b) to show your own levels of racial identity.

8

Contact: "I'm an innocent"

The Contact person often appears to be a vulnerable child with respect to racial issues. Unless one recognizes that ignorance permits racism to exist unchallenged and leaves the person for whom this schema is dominant in a psychologically fragile position, then it is tempting to leave such people uninformed about race and racism. These are some of the characteristics of the Contact schema:

- The person does not consciously think of herself/himself as White. When asked about his or her racial group, the person might respond in terms of his or her national group (Americans) or ethnicity (e.g., Italians).
- The person "discovers" that other racial groups exist. That is, even though the person may not have grown up in a completely racially segregated environment, he or she has somehow managed to avoid personal involvement with members of other racial groups until some personally significant encounter forces Persons of Color into the White person's awareness.
- The White person's interactions with members of other races are characterized by naiveté or timidity. The person thinks, for instance, that if he or she learns the slang of the group or wears the group's fashions or alters her or his physical appearance then he or she becomes a member of the group.
- The person claims to be color-blind and to ignore or minimize differences in treatment due to race. Thus, this person is likely to contend, "The only race that's important to me is the human race."

- The person believes that other groups necessarily want to be assimilated into White culture. Often the person will assume the role of "tour guide" of White culture to help the Person of Color acculturate.
- The person has minimal knowledge of other racial groups and cultures and believes that the White perspective should be applicable to all people.

The White person who uses Contact as a predominant schema has at least two options where personal identity development is concerned. He or she can avoid interracial contact and continue to believe that the world is a safe and fair place or she or he can befriend a Person of Color with the (not necessarily conscious) intent of learning what it is like to be Black or Asian or whatever.

The person who chooses the first option can continue to use Contact as long as her or his safe-haven is not violated by undeniable contradictory information. The person who chooses the second option, sooner or later, will discover that White society has rules about cross-racial interactions as do the societies of People of Color. The confusion resulting from the new awareness of either option signals the initiation of the next schema. The remedy for the Contact schema is more information and more exposure to cultural diversity.

The information quiz in Exercise 8.1, originally developed with the assistance of Ralph Piper and Maryam Jernigan, might help you get in touch with your level of information deficiency. Max Parker has suggested some activities (shown in Table 8.1) that might increase your exposure to other racial/cultural groups. As you participate in the activities, keep a diary of your reactions and others' reactions to you.

Exercise 8.1   Racial History Information Quiz

For each of the following items, circle the letter of the response that best answers the question. Answers are at the end of the exercise.

1. In 1988, many Japanese Americans received $20,000 in financial compensation from the U.S. government. They received this compensation _____.
   a.   because they were owed large tax refunds
   b.   as part of a trade deal with Japan
   c.   because they were interned in camps during World War II

    d.   as an apology by the U.S. government for the bombing of Hiroshima

2.   The Supreme Court case in 1954 that made school desegregation possible was _____.

    a.   Plessy vs. Ferguson

    b.   Sanchez vs. Grove City

    c.   Brown vs. Topeka

    d.   Bakke vs. California

3.   The reason why Native American (American Indian) reservations exist is because _____.

    a.   the Indians built them so that they could all stay together

    b.   the early settlers gave the land to the Indians

    c.   the early settlers killed many Indians and forced the rest to live there

    d.   they attract tourist trade

4.   Of the following, the group most responsible for building the national railroads is _____ Americans.

    a.   Chinese

    b.   African

    c.   Mexican

    d.   Native

5.   Benjamin Banneker was _____.

    a.   the undisputed heavyweight champ

    b.   a famous jazz singer

    c.   a New York civil rights activist

    d.   the designer of Washington, D.C.

6.   The African American inventor who developed the gas mask used in the Gulf War was _____.

    a.   Colin Powell

    b.   Garrett Morgan

    c.   George Washington Carver

    d.   Charles Drew

7.   Which of the following states was (were) originally part of Mexico? _____.

    a.   California

    b.   Louisiana

    c.   Texas

    d.   A & C

8. Most Black families are _____.
   a. lower class
   b. middle class
   c. upper middle class
   d. upper class

9. The group with the highest suicide rate in the country is _____.
   a. Whites
   b. Blacks
   c. Asians
   d. Hispanics

10. Approximately what percentage of the people in the US identify as White? _____
    a. 77%
    b. 13%
    c. 90%
    d. 50%

11. The racial group that has benefited most from affirmative action laws is _____.
    a. Whites
    b. Blacks
    c. Asians
    d. Latinx (Hispanics)

12. Who is Julian Cástro? _____
    a. a famous professional golfer
    b. an immigration lawyer
    c. the first Latinx governor in the United States
    d. a Latinx Presidential candidate

13. How many Asian Americans currently are justices on the Supreme Court? _____
    a. one
    b. two
    c. one and a half, if one counts the biracial justice who is completing another justice's term
    d. none

14. Clarence Thomas is _____.
    a. Secretary of State
    b. Attorney General of the United States

    c.   a Supreme Court Justice

    d.   Director of the Federal Bureau of Investigation (FBI)

Answers to the Quiz

1-c; 2-c; 3-c; 4-a; 5-d; 6-b; 7-d; 8-b; 9-a; 10-a; 11-a; 12-d; 13-d; 14-c.

    Just by guessing, you might have obtained a score of about three correct. Use the following categories to evaluate your knowledge of historical events.

    0–4   Uninformed

    5–9   Better than average

    10–14 Educated

If you had difficulty with the racial information quiz, here are some books that you might want to read to get a fuller and more personalized view of American history.

Brown, D. (1970). *Bury My Heart at Wounded Knee*. NY: Washington Square Press

Takaki, R. (1998). *Strangers from a Different Shore*. Boston: Little, Brown & Co.

Zinn, H. (1980). *A People's History of the United States*. NY: Harper & Row.

Rodriguez, R. (1982). *Hunger of Memory*. Boston: David Godine.

United State Census Bureau. https://www.census.gov/quickfacts/fact/table/US/PST045217.

TABLE 8.1 Examples of Contact Activities

of Activity: Observational	
Learning Task	Examples
List any new bits of knowledge you acquired	Attend movies or watch television shows that focus on racial/ethnic issues and/or racism

Type of Activity: Informational	
Learning Task	Examples
Compare accounts of social or historical events with your prior knowledge of these events	Read Asian, Black, Hispanic, Native American biographies and novels

TABLE 8.1 Continued

Read newspapers or magazines edited by marginalized groups of color

Enroll in a class focusing on racism or cultural issues

Type of Activity: Inter-group Contact

Learning Task	Examples
Notice customs and activities that match and/or differ from your experiences in similar White settings	Attend a restaurant specializing in other than European (White) food
	Attend a religious service in a community predominated by a racial/ethnic group other than Whites
	Attend a concert by an artist of another race

Note: The activities were adapted from Woodrow (Max) Parker's book, "Consciousness Raising."

9

Disintegration: "How can I be White?"

The second schema of the internalization of racism phase of White identity development is Disintegration. This schema is characterized by sometimes overwhelming feelings of guilt, shame, confusion, lack of a racial membership group to which one feels true kinship, and no socially approved guidelines for resolving one's internal turmoil.

This is the schema characterized by conscious acknowledgement of one's own Whiteness and recognition that being White has definite social implications. The most important of these implications is that if one is White, one is entitled to be treated better than if one is not. Failure to conform to racial socialization practices places the person's White entitlements at risk.

That this differential evaluation of people on the basis of skin color occurs in a country, based on the principle that all people are created equal (unless they are of color) is difficult for the White person to comprehend. In a country whose major religions advocate some versions of "Do unto others as you would have them do unto you," it is difficult for the White person to understand why "others" does not include People of Color.

Yet, seeking resolution from other White people of this internal turmoil is generally met with socialization into racism. One learns racism in the form(s) that it exists in one's most significant environments. The person learns that when interacting with People of Color, if he or she wants to be accepted by other Whites, then he or she at some time must violate virtually all of the moral and ethical principles that one tries not to violate with Whites.

Here are some of the ethical dilemmas the person must learn to resolve immorally in order to be White:

1. How can I be a moral or religious person and still be accepted by Whites who treat People of Color immorally?
2. How can I believe in freedom and equality without relinquishing White privilege?
3. How can I express love and compassion toward all people but keep People of Color at the bottom of the sociopolitical and economic hierarchies?
4. How can I say that I treat others with respect and dignity if I act as though People of Color are not worthy of such basic human concern?
5. How can I believe that people should be evaluated according to individual merits, but People of Color have no individual merits?
6. How can I be aware of injustice, but do nothing to correct it if it is racial?

And so the struggle goes. For many White people use of the Disintegration schema co-occurs with feelings of shame and guilt. Author Brené Brown defines *shame* as a debilitating set of emotions associated with the person's belief that he or she is personally flawed or bad, disconnected from humanity, and powerless to do anything to redeem one's self. Shame seems to occur for some Whites, whose identity is based on a core belief that they do not partake of White racism or privilege.

Consequently, when they are publicly revealed to have benefited from White privilege, on the inside, the person puts on what she or he believes is a poker face. Yet outside observers—especially People of Color—perceive it as a rigid mask of discomfort. Individuals hiding behind the mask either remain mired in the state of ambiguity associated with the Disintegration schema or they attempt to lessen their shame by using their Contact schema. Table 9.1 summarizes some of the ways that Disintegration is manifested in race-focused interactions.

TABLE 9.1 Some Examples of How White People Disintegrate

The Disintegration schema involves use of strategies that are self-protective.

To avoid being perceived as racist, the person avoids interracial interactions entirely.

"... with every interpersonal interaction I had across racial lines, I had been walking on eggshells with the People of Color on staff. I had been so excruciatingly careful to seem nonracist to People of Color that I was avoiding, closing off, distancing myself, that is, treating the People of Color on staff in an essentially racist manner" (Croteau, 1999, p. 30).

To cope with overwhelming feelings (possibly shame), the person withdraws from interactions, but not necessarily on purpose.

"I got overwhelmed and shocked by this stuff [discussions of White privilege] ... I couldn't really form a lot of opinions at once. I didn't really say anything because I was still ... I was bombarded by a lot of information" (Miller & Harris, 2007, p. 231).

Defensive anger directed towards People of Color and declaration of one's own oppressed status

"I never heard any acknowledgement that sometimes Black people have power, Black people have privilege, and Black people can be ignorant. That there are multiple power systems always enacted ... When we are asked to bring in an excuse for an absence for a holiday then the system is working against us [White Jews]. Black people who are Christians ... don't have to worry about getting Christmas off, because they already have it off. And they've never thought about that, and that's ignorance just in the way that Whites are ignorant" (Miller & Harris, 2007, p. 231).

Purposeful use of silence as a means of hiding

"I just sat back and listened because in my mind I was thinking I would have said something and probably would have stepped on somebody's toes. I just didn't want to get anybody upset" (Miller & Harris, 2007, p. 236).

Brené Brown defines *guilt* as feelings associated with realizing that one has behaved in a manner that is bad or flawed. Bad behavior is correctable. That is, that which has been learned can be unlearned. Guilt may cause the person to seek some empowering resolution to feelings of discomfort. As Audrey Thompson points out, guilt concentrates the White person's attention on oneself and the need to feel better. By feeling guilty about a situation that they cannot change, living in a racist society, people using Disintegration convince themselves that they have no responsibility for racism and, thus, they seek ways to restore their good feelings about themselves as White people without doing anything beyond feeling guilty.

The need to feel better may cause the White person to incorporate some version of a White-privilege distortion. Thus, the person internalizes some version of the belief that if Whites are advantaged, it is because they deserve to be. Conversely, if People of Color are disadvantaged, it is because they did not do enough to improve their status. This belief in White superiority and People of Color inferiority becomes the principle by which the person manages virtually all interactions in which race is an issue. Personal acceptance of this principle means that the person is resolving internal turmoil by becoming immoral. But more importantly, acceptance of this principle means that the person has chosen to be White in the limited ways her or his society offers.

It is difficult to be objective about oneself and one's circumstances when one's use of the Disintegration schema is dominant. Nevertheless, Exercise 9.1 may help you recognize the moral dilemmas as they occur in everyday life.

Exercise 9.1   Identifying Racial Moral Dilemmas

Racial moral dilemmas pit possible loss of the advantages of White privilege against one's sense of shared humanity. For each of the following situations, see if you can discover which of the moral dilemmas described on page 42 underlies the situation for the White persons involved in them.
Situations
1. The Latinx mayor of a large city wants to locate a shelter for the homeless in the only wealthy White district in the city (District 1). All of the other districts have one or more such shelters. Given that many of the residents of District 1 contribute their time and money to the poor People of Color in the inner city and the shelter will provide a refuge for these people, the mayor assumes that District 1 will be receptive to the plans for a shelter. Nevertheless, when the mayor's plan is announced, the residents strongly rebuke the mayor via litigation and negative publicity campaigns. Which dilemma is this? Why?
2. Fred, a White police officer, has always believed that he is "not a racist." However, Fred discovers that the department has instituted an affirmative action program whereby Whites and People of Color will take the same civil service examination, but will be promoted

---

according to separate lists. When Fred finds out that a Person of Color with a lower test score than his received the promotion he wanted, he files suit against the department, charging "reverse discrimination." Which dilemma is this? Why?

3. When Julia organizes a study group for her first-year law school classes, she does not even consider asking any of the People of Color in her class to join. If she had been asked why she did not, Julia would have said, "Since I didn't know any of my classmates very well, I approached the ones who looked most competent." Which dilemma is this? Why?

4. The last line of a White company's job-opening announcement is "The company encourages applications from qualified minorities." Which dilemma is this? Why?

5. George White is a flight instructor for a school from which most of the major airlines in the country recruit pilots. In most of these airlines, 100% of the pilots are White men. In Mr. White's classes, 100% of his students are White men. When a Black woman applies for admission to his school, he refuses her because, "if I train you, then chances are you'll get a job before I do." Which dilemma is this? Why?

Answers to Exercise 9.1

Although it is possible that more than one of the dilemmas pertains to each situation, here are some possibilities.

Situation 1: Dilemma #1. The residents' protestations seem to indicate that People of Color are worthy of basic human concern—only if it occurs at a distance. You might also recognize this as aversive racism.

Situation 2: Dilemma #2. Selection and placement exams typically are developed by White people and likely reflect White culture more so than other cultures. Thus, the White person enters the testing situation with a cultural advantage. Encouragement of freedom and equality in this case means finding ways to lessen the advantage. Yet lessening the advantage means individual White people must relinquish White privilege.

Situation 3: Dilemma #5. It appears that Julia believes that if people are of color, then they cannot also "look competent." In other words, she assumes lack of individual merit for an entire group(s) of people.

Situation 4: Dilemma #5. Why does the company specify that "minorities" must be qualified, but does not make the same specification for Whites? Perhaps it is assuming that Whites are naturally qualified and other racial groups are not.

Situation 5: Dilemma #2. Even though it is clear that White men dominate the pilot profession, Mr. White refuses to give one Person of Color the opportunity to become qualified because there might be one less opening for him—even though he already has a job!

Exercise 9.2   Personal Racial Moral Dilemmas

Now see if you can identify racial moral dilemmas in your own life. It sometimes helps if you try to recall the racial issues that make you uncomfortable. Write down the situations as they come to mind. Then use the descriptions on page 42 to help you uncover possible moral dilemmas. Recognition of the feeling states associated with your dilemmas might help you react to them in a way that feels self-empowering.

Describe Your Situation 1:

_____

_____

What dilemma is it? Why?

_____

_____

Circle the phrase or adjective that best describes how you feel in the situation:

No feelings Lonely Confused Guilty Ashamed Devastated Rejected Other

Describe Your Situation 2:

_____

_____

What dilemma is it? Why?

_____

_____

Circle the phrase or adjective that best describes how you feel in the situation:

No feelings Lonely Confused Guilty Ashamed Devastated Rejected Other

10

Reintegration: "We have the best because we are the best!"

The last schema of the internalization of racism phase, Reintegration, most closely approximates what White people mean when they profess their lack of racism. The general theme of this schema is idealization of Whites and White culture and denigration of Peoples of Color and their cultures.

This White superiority can be expressed overtly or covertly. For example, when your Uncle Tom tells a racist joke, he is actively expressing aspects of the Reintegration schema. If you do not challenge his humor, then you are covertly expressing Reintegration. Not disagreeing with racism perpetuates it.

General characteristics of people for whom the Reintegration schema is dominant are:

1. Hostility and anger directed toward People of Color;
2. Negative stereotypes of People of Color and exaggerated positive stereotypes of Whites when they are perceived as being "politically correct" (that is, operate according to the principle of white superiority);
3. Denial of any responsibility of White people for the problems of People of Color;
4. Fear of People of Color generally even though he or she may know none personally;
5. A primary focus on the enhancement of White privilege;
6. Achievements and accomplishments of People of Color are viewed as a personal threat;
7. Denial of the existence of racism in any form;

8. Minimizing of similarities between Whites and other racial groups; maximization of dissimilarities between Whites and others;
9. Whites are used as the penultimate standard for what is good, moral, and socially desirable;
10. Environmental information is distorted to conform to the White superiority principle;
11. Belief that Whites are no more racist than other groups.

A person who uses Reintegration as a dominant schema need not exhibit (either overtly or covertly) all of the characteristics listed. Demonstrating some of them strongly and consistently is sufficient.

The Reintegration schema is strongly represented in White society and may even be predominant, at least in some of its manifestations. In most White people's lives, socialization towards Reintegration attitudes seems to begin early in life. As soon as the child has been taught that there is a "them" (of Color) and a (White) "us," the stage has been set for ongoing development of Reintegration.

Moreover, Reintegration is a stable and consistent schema because cultural and institutional racism are so firmly established in American society. Thus, with only minimal psychic energy, the person can convince herself or himself that the reason why Whites are at the top of the sociopolitical hierarchy is not only because they are best, but also because members of the other racial groups are not trying hard enough or do not have sufficient abilities or skills. Efforts to inform people with high usage of this schema of systemic barriers is likely to earn one an unflattering label (e.g., "White liberal," "politically correct," "playing the race card"), but little else.

Given that persons for whom this schema is dominant do belong to the numerically and politically dominant racial group, it is usually possible for them to decide how they resolve issues raised in using the Reintegration schema. Two possibilities are: (1) they can purposefully avoid cross-racial interactions and thus maintain their Reintegration view of the world and/or (2) they may use this schema to gain a firmer conscious hold on their Whiteness.

If option 2 occurs, and the person is forced to exist in a multi-racial environment from which escape is not possible, and the person's stereotypic views of Whites and other racial groups are actively challenged (especially by White people), then the person may begin to build the foundation that permits development of the latter schemas. Since a crucial ingredient for encouraging abandonment of the Reintegration schema is White people's recognition and discouragement of their own and others' Reintegration beliefs and behaviors, it is important that one be able to recognize the subtle and not so subtle ways Reintegration can be expressed.

For each of the subsequent statements, use the following scale to indicate the extent to which you agree or disagree with it. Try to be as honest with yourself as possible.

1 = Strongly Disagree

2 = Disagree

3 = Agree and Disagree Somewhat

4 = Agree

5 = Strongly Agree

1. _____ Blacks complain too much about perceived racial injustices.
2. _____ Too many jobs that should be given to qualified Whites are given to unqualified Blacks.
3. _____ Blacks want too many special privileges.
4. _____ Black leaders have not assumed enough responsibility for ending racism in the Black community.
5. _____ If Black people want police officers to treat them fairly, they should not disobey the law.
6. _____ Blacks are more likely than Whites to prefer to live off welfare.
7. _____ Blacks are likely to be lazier than Whites.
8. _____ Whites are more intelligent than Blacks.
9. _____ Whites are less violence-prone than Blacks.
10. _____ Whites are more likely to be self-supporting than Blacks.

Scoring Procedures: Add together the numbered values of your responses to items 1 through 5. Then add your responses to items 6 through 10. You should have two scores.

The first items are similar to the ones used to measure symbolic racism. Symbolic racism is defined as sophisticated racism. In other words, stereotypes are implicit in the person's beliefs rather than overtly expressed.

The second score measures what McConahay calls "old fashioned racism." Old fashioned racism involves use of obvious, negative racial stereotypes.

Since most people cannot easily admit or recognize that they hold racist attitudes of any sort, it is difficult to say exactly what your scores mean. However, for each of your scores, you may use the chart below to obtain an estimate of your levels of these two kinds of attitudes. In the "old fashioned" and "symbolic" columns, place a check near the score range in which your score falls. If both of your checks occur on the same row, then you seem to have approximately equal levels of both kinds of attitudes; if your checks are on different rows, then one score (and presumably one type of racist attitudes) is higher than the other.

Score Range	Old Fashioned	Symbolic	Interpretation
9 or less	☐	☐	You have or admit to low levels of these attitudes; you're ready for the next chapter.
10 to 16	☐	☐	You have average levels of these attitudes. So, try to work through the next chapter.
17 or higher	☐	☐	You are probably an honest person, but your racial attitudes could use some work.

11

Pseudo-Independent: "Let's help them become more like Whites"

C apacity to use the Pseudo-Independence schema (that is, development of a high level of the attributes that characterize it) signals the first major movement toward development of a positive nonracist identity. Like the person who uses Reintegration as a dominant schema, the person using the Pseudo Independent schema tends to categorize White people as either "bad White people" or "good White people." Bad White people are those who engage in overt racist acts, whereas good White people are those whose intentions are good. Being perceived as a good White person is central to the person's self-concept and positive view of self when Pseudo Independence is his or her dominant schema. Some of the characteristics of Pseudo-Independence are as follows:

1. The person still believes that Whites and White culture are better than those of other racial groups, but not intentionally so. In fact, this person will often expend great effort in trying to figure out "environmental" explanations for why People of Color have not achieved at the same level as Whites without ever recognizing any worth in the environments from which the People of Color originate. Concepts such as "culturally deprived" and "broken homes" are typical of this schema.

2. The person can articulate principles of racial fairness, particularly as long as implementation of such principles have no immediate implications for the person's own life.

3. The person feels a responsibility for helping People of Color become more similar to Whites, though he or she may not consciously recognize that that is what he or she is attempting to do.

4. The person understands that White people are responsible for racism, but views it as a sin only of "deviant" Whites. He/she is unable to acknowledge any personal responsibility for it.

5. The person feels no responsibility for defining racism from a White perspective but rather depends on People of Color to reveal whether or not he or she is a racist.

6. This person can often recognize the ways in which he or she enjoys superior advantages relative to People of Color. However, he or she is likely to view the advantage gap as resolvable through the improved efforts of People of color.

7. "Pulling oneself up by one's bootstraps" is a philosophical principle of this schema. However, the Pseudo-Independent person expresses a desire to help the person acquire access to bootstraps, though he or she may never actually do anything to facilitate their acquisition;

8. He or she has friends who are People of Color. These "friends" are usually perceived to be similar to one's White friends or in need of some sort of help that the White person feels capable of providing.

9. This person shows an intellectualized interest in racial issues.

The Pseudo-Independent schema represents the person's attempt to recapture morality with respect to race. At least in part, he or she does this by "thinking" about racial issues rather than "feeling" about them. Thus, in a psychological sense the person remains aloof from racial issues even though he or she may appear to be actively advocating "liberal" perspectives with respect to such issues. So long as the person can remain aloof, so long as he or she remains personally untouched by racial events in her or his environments, then the Pseudo-Independent schema is a safe schema for the person to rely on.

Pseudo-independent people use a variety of strategies that permit them to maintain their racial comfort. Most of these strategies are designed to convince themselves that they can be White without also being bad, evil, or racist. These strategies also serve the incidental purpose of convincing other Whites that racism has virtually vanished. Therefore, People of Color who express other convictions are necessarily crazy, irrational, or old fashioned. Furthermore, if any remnants of racism do exist, they are not the responsibility of the White liberal person to resolve, given that the person believes that racial equality can be achieved even if racism does exist.

For the most part, Pseudo-Independent strategies focus on defining for People of Color how they should think, feel, and behave in order to be accepted by (White) society. Underlying the strategies often is a message to the Person of Color concerning how he or she should behave in order to allow the White person to continue to feel good about being White. Rarely do the strategies involve attempts to reeducate Whites about the meaning of being White in this country and/or the benefits that one receives as a partaker or transmitter of racism. Most Whites cannot articulate how they personally have benefited from racism. The Pseudo-Independent schema offers them protective cognitive strategies for not having to worry about emotionally charged issues. The strategies come in many forms. Not all people use all of the strategies. Here are some examples.

Talking past. This strategy is evoked when someone attempts to make the point that American society is not fair to People of Color—that society is not race neutral. The person with high levels of Pseudo-Independence becomes defensive and angry because a cherished belief is being challenged. So, in response, the person ignores, minimizes, or otherwise refuses to attend to the content of the communicator. Instead, he or she insists that things are better than they once were and attempts to use examples to prove the case. A person who is really adept at talking past will deflect responsibility for societal problems onto the person speaking.

The following dialogue illustrates talking past:

Black man: "I don't think Black people should be fighting this war. We've fought in every war this country has ever had and we've died in disproportionate numbers—all the time expecting that we'd get equal rights. Well, we never have and we won't this time! What's gonna be different after a four-year war that wasn't different before?"

White male politician: "I resent that! I resent that! I can't sit here and let you get away with making false statements like that. Black people have made a lot of progress since the 1960s. The highest military man in the country was a Black man. And you're depriving Black children of their dreams when you don't recognize the progress that your people have made."

Obviously, in this interaction, the politician does not want to attend to the issue of racial inequality. If he does, then he might bear some responsibility for doing something to change circumstances among White people. This of course, would be dangerous activity in terms of one's political future.

Role Model Selection. When a White person uses "talking past," the person might use a variety of examples or information to convince the communicator that he or she is delusional, but when the person uses "role model selection," he or she chooses a public figure to illustrate the communicator's thinking error. This strategy works especially well if the communicator herself or himself can be used as the exception that proves the communicator's logical errors.

Consider the following dialogue:

Asian American student leader: "Asian Americans are being discriminated against in the admissions process at this university. We're not being admitted in nearly the numbers that we should be when you look at our high school academic records."

White Administrator: "I don't know how you can say that. You're here and I understand that you're doing quite well here. Maybe someday you'll even be able to take over Professor Lee's job in the Engineering Department."

In this instance, Professor Lee is being used as "proof" that Asian students have equal opportunities at the university. The fact that the role model chosen to illustrate fairness has nothing to do with the topic under discussion seems to have escaped the administrator's attention.

Friendly Color-Blindness. The major issue here is that although the person believes herself or himself to be liberal and aware of racial injustices, he or she does not see them when they involve her or him.

White worker: "That was really a great meeting, wasn't it? We really got a lot done. I feel energized!"

Black worker: "I hated that meeting! Didn't you see how every time I said something, the whole group ignored me. But when a White person turned around and made the same comment I had just made, you all thought it was the greatest thing since white cheese. I'm getting sick of the racism that goes on around here."

White worker: "Oh, Rhonda. You're just being too sensitive. You know I pay attention to things like that and if something racist had been going on, I would have noticed it, wouldn't I?"

Besides being patronizing, the White worker communicates that her perception of whether racism exists is more accurate than the Black worker's. This strategy allows her to avoid personal responsibility for her part in the abusive situation.

The Real Victim. In this strategy, the person professes to have less freedom than People of Color and attributes this lack of freedom to People of Color. This strategy is illustrated in the following comments:

White male: "I noticed there's a sign posted on the bulletin board that's recruiting minorities for membership in a minority professional organization. If we White males advertised for members for White professional organizations, all hell would break loose."

OR

White female college student: "What does that sweatshirt saying mean? If we Whites started doing things like having high teas to show our culture, you minorities would make us feel guilty."

Aside from an absence of evidence that minorities would be upset by (positively) focused White cultural events, what these comments have in common is an assumption that if one does not say that an event is for Whites, then it is not. Most professional meetings in industry are for White males, whether they say so or not. The dominant culture in this country is White, whether Whites acknowledge it or not.

Ain't it a shame. The converse of friendly color-blindness is the "ain't it a shame" strategy. Here, the White person recognizes that racially discriminatory or derogatory behavior is occurring but does nothing to change the situation. In fact, the person may project the responsibility for addressing the problem to someone else. Here are two examples of "Ain't it a shame."

Mary: "I felt so uncomfortable when your Uncle Tom told those racist jokes at dinner tonight, Joe. And you just sat there! It's a shame you let him get away with stuff like that. Why didn't you say something to him?"

OR

> *White worker:* "I thought it was shameful the way Mr. Smith treated you in that meeting, Paula. He introduced all of the White panelists by their titles, "Dr. Whosit" but when he got to you, he just called you Paula. Everyone probably wondered why you were there. Why didn't you say something about it?"

This is a popular strategy because it allows the White person the illusion of sensitivity without requiring that he or she actually do anything about it.

Ancestor worship. This is a favorite strategy of individuals with dominant usage of Pseudo-Independence. This strategy has three components. It begins by identifying a White ethnic group (one's own or someone else's) who experienced discrimination somewhere in the world. The individual then expresses sympathy because, "After all my people have suffered, too." It ends by noting the present-day success of the abused White group as inspiration for the People of Color.

If you think about it, you can probably retrieve a number of examples in which you or a White acquaintance used ancestor worship, but here is an example to get you started.

> *White Corporate Executive:* "When my great grandfather came to this country, he had no money, he couldn't speak a word of English, and he was fleeing religious persecution. So, I understand how you people feel. But my family made it and so can you."

Can you tell why this strategy is particularly infuriating to People of Color? It is tantamount to ripping adhesive tape off of hairy skin. Generally at the time when such inspirational messages are offered, it is more than painful to the Person of Color to be reminded of her or his lack of opportunities relative to Whites whose ancestors have been in this country a much shorter time than those of most of the groups of Color.

I'm a racist. In this strategy, the person admits to racism for herself or himself as well as all other White people. That is, the person diffuses responsibility by assuming that he or she has no other alternatives since (in this person's eyes), "everyone is a racist."

A person who is adept at diffusion may be able to point out many reasons why he or she has no choice but to be a racist. "My parents were racists," "my friends would reject me if they thought I was disloyal to Whites," and so forth.

The person who uses this protective strategy may also be able to persuade herself or himself that the person is sorry about being a racist and is trying hard to change. However, what distinguishes the perspective of the person with high levels of Pseudo-Independence from persons with high levels of Immersion/Emersion is that the former can rarely identify anything specific that she or he personally has done that is wrong.

Advancement beyond an emphasis on Pseudo-Independent characteristics is not easy because the defensive strategies work so well and come in so many varieties. When progress occurs, it may be triggered by the ineffectiveness of one's favorite strategies in an emotionally charged racial atmosphere and/or personal awareness that one's manner of dealing with racial issues is inconsistent with how the person perceives herself or himself more generally. To the extent that either of these "triggers" is uncomfortable and unavoidable, then the arena is set for further racial identity development.

Because a primary characteristic of Pseudo-Independence is the capacity to separate intellect from emotions, the person tends to lose oneself in emotionally charged race-related situations, which is to say virtually any face-to-face interactions with race as a focus. That is, the person often is incapable of recognizing her/his real feelings at the time they are occurring. The following exercises attempt to help you recover and recognize those feelings.

Exercise 11.1   Rediscovering My Feelings about My Race

Think back to when you first became truly aware that you are White. Close your eyes and imagine yourself back in the situation. Try to feel what you felt at the time. Remember to focus on *yourself* rather than other people. Now write about your experience.

1.   Who was involved in the situation and what were their races?

_____

_____

---

2. What happened to you?

_____

_____

3. When that happened, you felt

_____

_____

4. Describe your bodily sensations at the time.

_____

_____

5. What did you do in response to your feelings or bodily sensations?

_____

_____

6. How did you feel about being White when this particular situation was over?

_____

_____

7. What did you learn about being White?

_____

_____

You may want to try this exercise several times, using experiences from different times in your life as the situation for analysis. Some things you can learn from your analysis are:

1. Your responses to the first question give you some clues as to who have been the most important people in helping you define your Whiteness. The person(s) whose viewpoints you adapted from the situation taught you some of the basics of how to be White.
2. Answers to the second question often reveal the content of the education you received with respect to your Whiteness. That is the situation taught you what to think about being White.
3. Question 3 responses are supposed to reveal the emotions you felt at the time. These are probably the same kinds of emotions that you learned to push out of awareness as you matured. Sometimes people have done so well at submerging and/or distorting these feelings that they cannot retrieve them for this exercise. If this is true of you, do not worry about it. With practice, you will be able to rediscover these feelings.
4. Examination of your bodily sensations in Question 4 provides information about how your body responds to your emotional state. Even when you have no conscious awareness of how you feel, your body probably knows. Become aware of these sensations so that you will recognize your feelings when you are in situations that feel racially charged to you.
5. Defensive strategies such as the ones described in this chapter evolve in response to strong emotions that cannot be managed otherwise. Your responses to Question 5 identify your favorite strategies. They may be similar to those I have described; they may be different. Learn to recognize when you are using a defensive strategy rather than actively focusing on the situation as it is occurring.
6. No matter how hard you tried, it was probably difficult to focus on your racial group membership rather than someone else's. Nevertheless, you do leave situations such as the one you have described with some definite feelings about being White. Question 6 helps you pinpoint these feelings. Probably you have similar feelings about yourself as a White person even now.
7. People engage in self-talk. Self-talk can help you feel better about yourself or worse. Your responses to Question 7 show how you communicate with yourself about being White. Do the things you learned help you feel better or worse?

Refer back to your analyses of yourself in the previous exercise. Ideally it provided some ideas about how you react to your Whiteness on a daily basis. Let us see if it did. In this activity, you are to keep a daily diary in which you record your experiences of being consciously White. Try keeping the diary for about a week then compare your self-analyses of Exercise 11.1 to the themes that occur in your diary.

To structure your diary, in addition to the questions raised in Exercise 11.1, also respond to the following:

1. How did the situation turn out?
2. How did I want it to turn out?
3. What did I do (or could I have done) to make the situation come out as I wanted it to?

12

Immersion/Emersion: "I'm White!"

Does one or more of the following characteristics describe you?

- I feel an almost overwhelming anger when I see how other White people—even friends and family—deal with racial issues.

- I think I am more knowledgeable about racial matters than most White people I meet.
- I find myself searching for other White people who think about race in the way that I do.
- I participate in discussion groups to help me learn how to be White better.
- I notice both positive and negative things about being White that I never noticed before.

If your answer is yes, then you are likely experiencing some aspects of the Immersion/Emersion schema. The Immersion/Emersion schema is the lens through which the person actively attempts to redefine the meaning of Whiteness in this society. In other words, the individual attempts to be White in a way that "feels" right and moral.

Distinguishing Immersion/Emersion from Pseudo-Independence is sometimes rather subtle. The primary difference between the two is that the latter still localizes race and racial tensions in People of Color whereas Immersion/Emersion users recognize the contributions of Whites in such matters. Use of the Immersion/Emersion schema requires the person to focus a critical lens on Whiteness rather than hiding behind the fiction of helping the disadvantaged "Racial Other." Table 12.1 uses updated questions from a widely publicized national poll to illustrate the difference between Pseudo-Independent and Immersion/Emersion perspectives.

Most White people do not use this White racial identity schema very much. That is, it rarely becomes a dominant schema. The Immersion/Emersion schema requires one to assume personal responsibility for racism and to understand one's role in perpetuating it. Try Exercise 12.1 to get a sense of what I mean by the concept of taking personal responsibility. Perhaps more importantly, however, it requires the person to face the feelings of guilt, anger, and anxiety that were pushed out of awareness during the internalization-of-racism phase of White identity development. This process of being brutally honest with oneself is painful and so most people would rather avoid it if they can.

The self-discovery process might not be quite so hard to undertake if the rewards for doing so were more evident; that is, if Whites could see more nonconflicted, nonracist White people, they might feel more comfortable and hopeful about redefining themselves. Unfortunately, however, most people who progress far enough in their identity development to begin thinking about what kind of White person they would like to be frequently must answer this question on their own and generally in isolation. Other Whites often feel threatened by the White identity self-seeker because painful memories are revived. People of Color typically feel threatened by this person's overt interest in Whiteness because, in their sociopolitical experiences, "White" people talking about being White generally have not had benevolent goals in mind.

Although in my book, *Black and White Racial Identity: Theory, Research, and Practice,* I hypothesize that the process of identifying racism and discovering one's own Whiteness are both phases of the Immersion/Emersion schema, the processes probably do not happen independently. That is, individuals will find themselves struggling with both kinds of issues. Nevertheless, it is not hard to recognize a person who has arrived at some degree of resolution of Immersion/Emersion issues.

Resolving Immersion/Emersion issues involves an intensive and extensive examination of oneself as well as other Whites and White culture. Often people using this schema engage in a variety of self-exploration activities such as reading autobiographies of White people who have engaged in similar explorations, family discussions about race, and consciousness raising groups. Each of the activities has a four-pronged focus—understanding, recognizing, and accepting White culture and distinguishing White culture from racism.

The strong and multiple feelings that are aroused within this schema generally catch their hosts by surprise. Two of the more powerful of these feelings are anger and embarrassment. Each of these feelings can be directed against other Whites as well as oneself.

Anger can be aroused when the person becomes aware of the extent to which he or she has been taken in by the "White lie" (discussed in Chapter 3). The person may be angry at himself or herself for being so gullible; he or she may also be angry at the people considered to have participated in the conspiracy to distort the realities of race. Exercise 12.2 will help you locate one impetus for your anger—familial expressions of anger.

One's level of embarrassment generally rises as the person becomes aware of her or his own previous social ineptness with respect to race as well as that of other White people. When this affective condition occurs, the person may become socially inhibited because of continuous self-doubt, self-questioning, and reluctance to be perceived as inept.

High levels of empathy for oneself and other Whites are generally not automatically stimulated when people have strong Immersion/Emersion characteristics. These individuals tend to be quite critical of themselves and others. This new criticalness is positive because it suggests that the persons are using analytical skills to overcome their lifelong socialization (See Exercise 12.3).

Carried to the extreme, however, criticalness can also have negative consequences. People tend to dislike, avoid, and feel uncomfortable around people who are forever criticizing them. Thus, in addition to possibly not liking oneself very much for the moment, the person may feel abandoned or let down by her or his racial group.

As the Emersion phase of this schema develops, the person is likely not only to *feel* isolated and abandoned by friends, family, and peers, but also actually to be abandoned. At this point in her or his development, the newly defined White person cannot help testifying and attempting to convert other Whites. Most of the potential converts will have no idea what the revivalist means by "internalizing racism" and "redefining one's own Whiteness."

People tend to respond with fear to those things that they do not understand. The topic of race relations summons a particularly frightening set of issues in these days and times. Other White people will observe a member of their group dealing with such issues frankly, and it will frighten them. People express fear differently. Sometimes it will masquerade as anger or discomfiture or aversion. Chances are the people who love you best initially will have the strongest negative reactions to the new you.

It sometimes helps to lessen the pain of rejection to remind oneself that the source of the unusual reactions one elicits while this schema is developing is usually fear. Then, particularly if the person involved is someone you care about and/or who cares about you, imagine them as a frightened child. For the moment, think about them and react to them as though they are that child. This strategy will not necessarily guarantee that the other person's racial identity development will be enhanced. However, it may help you to not take their reactions too seriously and consequently to maintain faith in yourself.

A little empathy goes a long way. Developing a nonracist White identity is hard work—particularly when one is doing it on one's own. It also sometimes is scary. A graduate student I know describes the experience as venturing out on a flimsy branch without being sure that you can come back to a more solid limb or that the branch you have chosen will support you. Reminding oneself of how hard the growth process is and congratulating oneself when progress occurs makes it easier to accept others who are engaged in the struggle. It also makes it easier for you to continue to grow.

Lest it sound like Immersion/Emersion is no fun, it does have some enriching aspects. Not the least of these is its self-liberating qualities. When one is no longer defined by external criteria, one can begin to see humor in White culture. When one defines oneself, one can no longer be coerced into being someone else via guilt, fear, and so forth. When one knows that one is White, one can begin to enjoy different aspects of White culture and claim it as one's own. Exercise 12.4 will help you focus on some of the fun in being a nonracist White.

TABLE 12.1 How Immersion/Emersion Differs from Pseudo-Independence

Column 1 Pseudo-Independent Items	Column 2 Immersion/Emersion Items
Would Black Americans benefit if the following took larger leadership roles? Stacy Abrams Corey Booker Clarence Thomas Maxine Waters	Would White Americans better understand their role in promoting racial tensions if the following took larger leadership roles? Nancy Pelosi Mike Pence Bernie Sanders Mitch McConnell
Would a Democratic administration do more to help blacks [sic] get ahead, or would it not be much different from the current Republican administration?	Would a Democratic administration do more to help Whites dismantle institutional racism or would it not be much different from the current Republican administration?

TABLE 12.1 Continued

Do you believe that because of past discrimination against black [sic] people, qualified blacks [sic] should receive preference over equally qualified whites [sic] in such matters as getting into college or getting jobs?	Do you believe that because they are White, qualified Whites should receive preference over equally qualified Blacks in such matters as getting into college or getting jobs?
Is there enough legislation on the books to improve conditions for blacks [sic] in this country, with further progress coming through private efforts? Or is there more legislation needed?	Is there enough legislation on the books to compel Whites in this country to treat Blacks fairly, with further progress coming through the efforts of individual Whites? Or is more legislation needed?
Can fairness in education, hiring, and promotion be accomplished without quotas?	Can fairness in education, hiring, and promotion be accomplished without ending White Privilege?

Note: *The questions in Column 1 were taken from a Newsweek poll (May 6, 1991). Names have been updated when necessary to be more contemporary.*

Exercise 12.1 Taking Personal Responsibility for Your White Privilege

By now, you know that maintaining White privilege merely requires you to live your life as many White people do; pay no attention to the ways in which they benefit from racism! Still others believe that racism and privilege are so ingrained in the system that nothing any White person does can change it. This exercise is about acknowledging privilege as it occurs in your life, figuring out what systemic factors maintain it, and developing a plan to change it should you so desire.

Make a list of the ways in which White privilege is present in your everyday life. Then try to figure out what racism principle maintains it (see Chapter 6). Think of some possible ways you might counteract each of the individual privileges that you list; in other words, speculate about how you might take personal responsibility. Here is an example of what I would like you to do.

Privilege: I live in a neighborhood where all of my neighbors are White.

Racism Principle: I think this is a case of housing discrimination. I don't think real estate agents show houses in this neighborhood to People of Color. I don't think my neighbors want them to.

Taking Personal Responsibility: I could move to a more racially diverse neighborhood. I could report real estate agents to the local housing authorities if I think that they are illegally steering People of Color away from my neighborhood. I could talk to my neighbors about how integrating the neighborhood would make it a more interesting place.

Now it's your turn.

Privilege:

Racism Principle:

Taking Personal Responsibility:

You might want to try this exercise more than once. After analyzing the privilege, it is important to determine the barriers to your taking personal responsibility. So, the person in the example said the following:

Barriers to Taking Personal Responsibility: I like where I live. I don't want to make my neighbors angry at me. I don't want to be responsible for the real estate agent losing her job. She was very nice to me.

Of course, you recognize the person's barriers as excuses for not giving up privilege. However, ultimately, the individuals will have to decide whether the benefits still feel as good when they interface with systemic racism.

Exercise 12.2   When I Get Angry, I …

In our society, we are taught to be afraid of our anger and to push it out of sight. If one is White, one is socialized to be rational rather than emotional. Nevertheless, anger can be a powerful energizer for change both inside oneself and in the world more broadly. But to use it effectively, one must be able to recognize it when it is aroused. Recognition and expression are not synonyms. If one recognizes one's anger, one can decide how or whether to express it.

First, let us examine how you think and feel about anger in general.

1. How was anger expressed in your family?

2. What messages did you learn in your family regarding your own anger?

3. When I get angry, I

4. When someone is angry at me, I

5. The thing that frightens me most about being angry is

6. The thing that frightens me most about someone being angry at me is

Now analyze your answers for self-talk and themes. Recall that you learned how to do that in Chapter 11. Answers to questions 1 and 2 are most clearly related to self-talk or what goes on inside your head when you are angry. Answers 3 and 4 likely describe how you act in situations in which anger is evident. The barriers that interfere with your capacity to channel anger effectively perhaps are revealed by your answers to questions 5 and 6.

It is important to recognize the impetus for your anger in race-related interactions.

Think of a White person you know whose manner of dealing with race makes you angry. List as many characteristics of this person who makes you angry as you can.

The things about _____'s (fill in a name) way of dealing with race that make me angry are:

Traits	Your Ideal
_____	_____
_____	_____
_____	_____
_____	_____

Go through your list and circle the characteristics that are (or were) characteristics you share. Very often, when we are angry at people because of the way they are, we are really angry at ourselves for being the way we are. If you circled any of the traits you listed, then use your anger to help you change the traits you do not like.

Next to the traits you circled, write a brief description of how you would like to be with respect to this trait (your ideal). Then use your anger to energize your movement toward your ideal. When you are angry at someone because of one of "your" traits, do something to express your ideal.

The most difficult anger to manage is cross-racial. A situation is cross-racial if it actually includes people of races other than your own. It is also implicitly cross-racial if it involves Whites talking about or making decisions about these groups. In such situations, all of the aspects of your anger that you discovered in the beginning of this exercise are likely to be clamoring for attention, most of the time unbeknownst to you. Try to anticipate how the aspects of your anger will appear in the following potentially tense situations.

1. Someone of color accuses you of being a racist.
2. An important White person belittles your interest in diversity and says, "You'll outgrow it."
3. Someone of color calls you a racial epithet.
4. Someone White accuses you of being a "White liberal" (or worse) because of your views on race and race relations.
5. People of Color laugh at you when you tell them that you are participating in a White consciousness group.

One strong feature of people with high levels of Immersion/Emersion characteristics is their ability to analyze racial situations for their implications for Whites as well as People of Color (if they are involved). A second is their willingness to reeducate other Whites about being White. In the situations that follow, see if you can explain how the situation hurts Whites as well as People of Color.

> **Situation 1:** During the last week in February, a White fraternity decides to have a White history week. One of the highlights of the week is a slave auction, the proceeds from which will be donated to charity.

1. Why would People of Color find this offensive?

2. Why should Whites find it offensive?

3. If you were the fraternity advisor, how would you help the members learn to be positively White?

> **Situation 2:** Several White workers wear confederate flag lapel pins to work one day to show "group solidarity." The two Black workers in the company complain to the (White male) supervisor about them and the next day he wears a confederate flag to work.

1. Why were the Black workers upset?

2. Why should the White non-pin wearers have been upset?

3. What could the White non-pin wearers have done to "de-fuse" this situation?

> **Situation 3:** The sports teams in several cities are named after American Indians (e.g., "redskins," "chiefs," "braves"). Although many members of these groups have protested what they consider to be derogatory stereotypes, the teams have ignored their protests.

1. What is the adverse impact on Whites in this situation?

2. What is the adverse impact on the American Indians in this situation?

3. How would you intervene to resolve intergroup tensions in this situation if you were the sports commissioner?

> **Situation 4:** You read in your local newspaper that the infant mortality rate of certain groups of color is more than twice that of Whites.

1. How does this situation harm Whites?

2. What does it reveal about the circumstances of these groups of color?

3. What responsibility do Whites bear for this situation?

Exercise 12.4 White Culinary Challenge

Plan a White dinner. The rules for this dinner are that the food served must be white and come from White culture. Guests who are invited must wear clothing from White culture (ethnic dress permitted), and bring a story about growing up White in America.

Use the Exercise to help you think about the value of diversity and to learn more about White history from a personal perspective.

13

Autonomy: "I see color and like it!"

The last schema of White identity development is Autonomy. When using this schema, the person attempts to interact with the world and commune with himself or herself from a positive White, nonracist perspective. That is, the person is committed to being White, has an ideal view of what a nonracist White person is like, and is continually involved in the process of engaging in those activities and life experiences that will move the person toward her or his ideal.

It is important to think about the Autonomy schema as a lifelong process of discovery and recommitment to defining oneself in positive terms as a White person. What makes this schema markedly different from the earlier schemas is that when the person is capable of using it consistently, he or she has a more realistic, personally meaningful view of Whiteness that can be nurtured, internalized, and taken out and examined when it appears not to be working as the individual would like.

Autonomy is also a schema by which the person truly values diversity. Thus, he or she actively seeks out opportunities to increase the racial diversity in her or his life because the person recognizes that she or he can learn and grow from such experiences. Persons with high levels of this schema do not rely on People of Color to define Whiteness for them or to validate for them their "nonracist" status. Rather, these are questions that the individual asks of herself or himself and answers in a manner that feels personally comfortable given the overall self-concept that the person has.

Working toward the elimination of sociopolitical oppression in general is a strong characteristic of high levels of usage of the Autonomy schema. Via one's own self and environmental examination, the person becomes increasingly aware of the many shapes and shades in which oppression can exist. He or she also attempts to understand how oppression hurts all people even when someone else is its focus. Thus, for instance, if racism or sexism hurts someone else today, persons for whom Autonomy is the dominant schema understand that they also hurt themselves (perhaps) in less direct ways and that what is indirect today can easily become direct tomorrow.

Lest it sound like the person with high levels of usage of the Autonomy schema characteristics is a paragon of virtue, let me suggest that this is not necessarily the case. If the person was a paragon before he or she embarked on the road to White racial identity development, then he or she will likely remain so if the journey is ever finished.

Likewise, if the person was less than a paragon prior to the journey, he or she, too, will probably remain so. Development of a healthy White identity does not make one a perfect human being. It merely helps free one to potentially enjoy oneself and the society of a variety of human beings who will appear in many colors.

Nor will environmental obstacles necessarily disappear as the person becomes more Autonomous. Your in-laws will still be your in-laws. Your taxes will still be due on April 15. And if you had no unusual talents before you began developing Autonomy characteristics, then it is quite unlikely that any will appear magically as a result of your becoming more Autonomous.

Even though developing your White racial identity is not a cure all, it does offer the possibility of a better you in the area of race and race relations. Exercises 13.1 and 13.2 will help you examine how far you have advanced in this regard.

Autonomy is sometimes called the schema of "racial self-actualization." This means that a moral definition of Whiteness has become a stable and central component of who the person is. Racial self-actualization shares many of the characteristics that Abraham Maslow postulated as components of healthy development more generally speaking. Below is a list of characteristics that might describe the securely White (Autonomous) person. Place a check beside the ones that describe you.

_____   1.   Spontaneity: The capacity to respond in race-related situations without being debilitated by fears of being perceived as a "racist" or "a_____" (supply your own emotionally charged racial epithet).

_____   2.   Problem centered rather than self-centered: The ability to focus on resolving the racial issue at hand rather than immobilizing oneself with fears about one's own inadequacies or someone else's.

_____   3.   Autonomous and independent: The capacity to follow one's own heart even when those Whites you value most might reject you.

_____   4.   Original appreciation of people of various races and culture: The capacity to enjoy people for what you see in them rather than for society's stereotypes of what you ought to see.

_____   5.   "Spiritual quest" for your racial identity: Frequently, development of a strongly Autonomous personality with respect to racial identity is preceded by a seemingly abrupt change in one's way of viewing life roughly akin to a religious rebirth.

_____   6.   Identification with all humankind: The recognition that no racial group is superior (or inferior) and the commitment to make one's own share of the world a better place for all people regardless of their race.

_____ 7.   Intimate friendships: The ability to have strong personal relationships with a few "special" people whose specialness is your mutual interests, values, and beliefs rather than your race(s).

_____ 8.   Realistic perspective: The ability actually to hear and see what is happening when race is an issue rather than distorting circumstances to assuage your fears or conform to stereotypes.

_____ 9.   Sense of Humor: The capacity to use philosophical and creative humor rather than hostile and stereotypic humor in stressful and nonstressful racial situations.

_____ 10.   Resistance to racial conformity: The will to resist others' definitions of your Whiteness when they do not match your own self-definition.

_____ 11.   Proactive rather than reactive interactions with one's environment: The willingness to confront "racial problems" before they become problems and to propose equitable resolutions for them.

_____ 12.   Humanistic values behaviors and attitudes: A perspective in which people, regardless of color, are considered to be equally valuable and important.

_____ 13.   Self-acceptance: The capacity to accept oneself as a White person and to allow the racial part of oneself to influence other aspects of one's life.

_____ 14.   Acceptance of others: The recognition, acceptance, and valuing of the similarities and differences among and within Whites as well as Peoples of Color.

_____ 15.   Self-integration: The capacity to accept race as one aspect of who you (and others) are rather than the totality of oneself.

An important aspect of Autonomy is the person's understanding that acceptance of one's own Whiteness and others' races cannot occur in a racial vacuum. It is easy to express seemingly Autonomous views when they have no implications for how one lives one's life. But the truly Autonomous person wants her or his racial views to impact his or her own life and takes action to ensure that they do.

Your task in this exercise is to analyze the racial diversity in your life by answering the following questions:

1a. What percentage of your neighbors are People of Color?

1b. How much intimate contact do you have with your neighbors of Color?

1c. What can (or did) you do to increase the racial diversity of your neighborhood?

2. How many of your current friends are White (check one)

_____ All of them

_____ Half or more

_____ Less than half

_____ None

3a. Use the racial identity schemas to describe the racial climate of your work or school environment?

3b. Why are you satisfied or not satisfied with the racial climate?

3c. What have (or can) you do to improve the climate?

3d. At what cost?

4. What are Autonomous answers to questions 1 through 3d?

Answers

You are on your own now! By the time you have reached this point in your development, your answers undoubtedly are much better than any I could generate.

14

Using Racial Identity Schemas to Understand Daily Events

You have and will encounter reactions to your attempts to define positive Whiteness. They will come in many forms. Sometimes reactions to my efforts come in the form of commentaries related to something that I have written. The excerpts that I share with you are from people who wrote to me personally, although I am not using their names. Here goes.

> In response to, my op-ed on White heterosexual male privilege (WHMP),[1] a White man wrote:
>
> "You are nothing but a POS!"
>
> Another wrote:
>
> "I am a 55 white male. I have a BA and 149 IQ but have spent my whole adult life working at menial jobs. No one would hire me because I am white. I had to work to get the BA no scholarships no loans. They said because I was white I got no help.
>
> Now what I ask madam is how do I access this privledge [sic]. You say it exists and I belive [sic] you. So how do I get my share [sic]."

---

[1] Helms, J. E. (2016). An Election to Save White American Male Privilege. https://www.bc.edu/content/dam/files/schools/lsoe_sites/isprc/pdf/Helms%20LPT%202016%20(1).pdf

In response to my observations about White professors teaching about race, a White male professor wrote:[2]

> As a WHMP[,] I have taken seriously your question of "Why would White people relinquish the power of Whiteness?" and have perhaps at least one answer to that question: to regain their humanity. What I mean by this is that White people have lost their humanity, if not from the way they themselves directly behave towards People of Color, from their inaction in situations where People of Color are treated inhumanely. This inaction of course perpetuates White privilege, making it difficult to say that "inaction" is truly inaction. What saddens me is that the opportunity to restore their humanity might not be enough motivation for some White people to go through the painful process of change, including their own loss of privilege.

Actually, similar commentaries have always been out there, but perhaps you are more attuned to them now and have a rationale for understanding the speakers/writers better. If you have come this far by grappling with your own racial identity issues, you should be able to analyze these men's comments and decide how they feel as well as how you feel about the comments. You should also be able to identify the schemas each person is using, figure out which of your schemas it arouses, and decide how you might engage in conversation with the person. Remember that opportunities to influence racial dialogues are often unexpected; so think of this as three of the many opportunities you will have to practice using racial identity skills.

---

[2] Helms, J. E. (2017). The challenge of making Whiteness visible: Reactions to four Whiteness articles. *The Counseling Psychologist, 45*, 717–726.

Epilogue

Once, after I had lectured on White identity at a predominantly White, coeducational Ivy League college in the northeast, a White male junior asked me, "Why should I spend time trying to develop a healthy White identity? Don't I have more important things to do—like graduating and getting into law school and having a family?" At the time, his question seemed nonsensical to me. After all, I reasoned from my humanistic orientation, does not every reasonable person want to be the best person one can be?

However, in retrospect, I hear his question in a different light. It seems to me that he was asking me to resolve a larger existential question: What has the average White person to gain by risking privilege, predictability, and stability in life merely for the sake of positive White identity? What *is* the payoff? I suspect that I did not have a convincing answer for the young man's question at that time. Nor am I sure that I have one now. But to me development of a positive White identity means:

- the White person can look in the mirror and like and respect the reflected person;
- the White person can look in the mirror and see a White person without also seeing guilt, anger, and confusion;
- the White person can know that he or she obtained privileges and benefits from society because he or she "was qualified" rather than because she or he is the "best" color;
- the White person can approach the world from a mentally healthy perspective rather than having to deny, distort, or avoid the realities of the world;

- the White person can learn to pity those who can only love themselves by hating others;
- the White person can be a person who does not survive via hatred;
- the White person will be a more complete human being.

Perhaps these goals are not worth the risk. Perhaps they are. Unfortunately, one can never know which alternative is true if one does not begin the growth process. So, growthful journey!

References

These are the resources that I found directly or indirectly useful in writing this book.

Axelson, J. (1985). *Counseling and development in a multicultural society.* Pacific Grove, CA: Brooks / Cole.

Bergerson, A. A. (2003). Critical race theory and white racism: Is there room for White scholars in fighting racism in education? *Qualitative Studies in Education, 16,* 51–63.

Blustein, D. L. (2006). *The psychology of working: A new perspective for career development, counseling, and public policy.* Mahway, NJ: Lawrence Erlbaum Associates.

Brown, B. (2006). Shame resilience theory: A grounded theory study on women and shame. *Families in Society: The Journal of Contemporary Social Services, 87,* 43–52.

Cress-Welsing, F. (1990). *The Isis papers.* Chicago, IL: Third World Press.

Croteau, J. M. (1999). One struggle through individualism: Toward an antiracist White racial identity. *Journal of Counseling & Development, 77,* 30–32.

Eichstedt, J. L. (2001). Problematic White identities and a search for racial justice. *Sociological Forum, 16,* 445–467.

Gaertner, S. L., & Davidio, J. F. (2005). Understanding and addressing contemporary racism: From aversion racism to the common in group identity model. *Journal of Social Issues, 61,* 615–639.

Hardiman, R. (1982). *White identity development: A process-oriented model for describing the racial consciousness of White Americans.* Unpublished doctoral dissertation, University of Massachusetts, Amherst, MA.

Helms, J. E. (1990). *Black and White racial identity: Theory, research and practice.* Westport, CT: Greenwood Press.

Helms, J. E., & Cook, D. A. (1999). *Using race and culture in counseling and psychotherapy: Theory, research, and process.* Boston, MA: Allyn & Bacon.

Jones, J. (1972). *Prejudice and racism.* Reading, MA: Addison Wesley.

Katz, J. H. (1978). *White awareness: Handbook for anti-racism training.* Norman, OK: University of Oklahoma Press.

Liu, W. M. (2002). The social class-related experiences of men: Integrating theory and practice. *Professional Psychology: Research and Practice, 33,* 355–360.

Liu, W. M., Ali, S. R., Soleck, G., Hopps, J., Dunston, K., & Pickett, Jr., T. (2004). Using social class in counseling psychology research. *Journal of Counseling Psychology, 51,* 3–18.

Maslow, A. H. (1968). *Toward a psychology of being.* Princeton, NJ: Van Nostrand.

McConaghy, J. B., & Hough, J. C., Jr. (1976). Symbolic racism. *Journal of Social Issues, 32,* 23–45.

Miller, A. N., & Harris, T. M. (2005). Communicating to develop White racial identity in an interracial communication class. *Communication Education, 54,* 223–242.

Neville, H. A., Lilly, R. L., Duran, G., Lee, R. M., & Browne, L. (2000). Construction and initial validation of the Color-Blind Racial Attitudes Scale (CoBras). *Journal of Counseling Psychology, 47,* 59–70.

Parker, W. M. (1988). *Consciousness-raising: A primer for multicultural counseling.* Springfield, IL: Charles C Thomas.

Painter, N. I. (2010). *The history of White people.* New York: W.W. Norton and Company.

Phinney, J. S. (1990). Ethnic identity in adolescents and adults: Review of research. *Psychological Bulletin, 108* (3), 499–514.

Sternberg, R. J., Grigorenko, E. L., & Kidd, K. K. (2005). Intelligence, race, and genetics. *American Psychologist, 60,* 46–59.

Takaki, R. (1998). *Strangers from a different shore: A history of Asian Americans.* New York: Penguin Books.

Thompson, A. (2003). Tiffany, friend of People of Color: White investments in antiracism. *Qualitative Studies in Education, 16,* 7–29.

Your Personal Journey with A Race Is a Nice Thing to Have

This and the following page can serve as your journal of personal reactions to each chapter of this book. After you have completed each chapter, ask yourself the following questions and then record your answers on these pages or on your own paper.

- What single point struck you as most important or useful in the chapter?
- Did the text or the exercises raise any emotional issues for you?
- What are you going to do about this knowledge and the emotions brought out by the chapter?

CPSIA information can be obtained
at www.ICGtesting.com
Printed in the USA
BVHW092226100621
609158BV00002B/67